PORTRAITS OF CHILDFREE WEALTH

26 STORIES ABOUT HOW BEING CHILDFREE
IMPACTS YOUR LIFE, WEALTH AND FINANCES

JAY ZIGMONT, PHD, CFP®

CONTENTS

Acknowledgments   v

Introduction   vii

1. Alison – A Portrait of Freedom   1
2. Amelia and Matt – A Portrait of Freedom   8
3. Aurora – A Portrait of Getting Started   17
4. Autumn – A Portrait of Too Many Choices   21
5. Betty – A Portrait of Starting Over   28
6. Carly – A Portrait of Struggle   34
7. Cathryn – A Portrait of Fear   40
8. Cindy – A Portrait of Caring   47
9. Greg – A Portrait of Logic and FIRE   53
10. Gustavo – A Portrait of Worry   57
11. Heather – A Portrait of Persistence   63
12. Jacy – A Portrait of Compromise   70
13. Jesse – A Portrait of Intentional Balance   77
14. Josie – A Portrait of Being Lost   83
15. Kristi – A Portrait of Freedom and Practicality   89
16. Kristina – A Portrait of a Cat Lady   96
17. Laura – A Portrait of Stability   101
18. Lorna – A Portrait of Accidental FIRE   109
19. Maggie – A Portrait of Strength   117
20. Maria – A Portrait of Getting Started   126
21. Michelle – A Portrait of Good Vibes   130
22. Mirena – A Portrait of Options   137
23. Molly and James – A Portrait of Love   142
24. Rebekah and Matthew – A Portrait of Recentering   150
25. Ryan A – A Portrait of Freedom and No Regrets   158
26. Ryan G – A Portrait of Successful Laziness   165
27. Appendix A – Research Plan and Interview Questions   172
28. Appendix B: FILE vs. FIRE   177
29. Appendix C: The Gardener and the Rose   181

About the Author   185

For information about this title or to order other books and/or electronic media,
contact the publisher:

Childfree Wealth

Water Valley, MS

coachdrjay@gmail.com

https://www.childfreewealth.com

Library of Congress Control Number: 2022907253

ISBN: 978-1-945050-02-2

Printed in the United States of America

ACKNOWLEDGMENTS

I need to give a special thanks to all who participated in this book. It is genuinely your book, and I am just a narrator. You shared your life story and the impact of being Childfree on your life, wealth, and finances. You shared more than I could have ever expected and to you, and I can't say thanks enough.

Thanks to my Editor Ashley Maready and all of my Beta Readers

And as always, thanks to my wife, who puts up with my craziness.

INTRODUCTION

This book is a collection of 26 stories about Childfree Wealth, Life, and Finances. I call each of the stories a portrait as it is a snapshot of life, not intended to be all-inclusive. There is no way I could do anyone's life story justice and have it fit within this book. To that end, I tried to focus on what is important to my interviewees and the impact that being Childfree had on them. You will find extraordinary stories in this book that inspire you and make you cry. Some portraits challenged my assumptions and provided support for my own choices.

To create the stories, each person (or couple) met with me for an interview of about an hour via Zoom. For research nerds, you can find my research plan and interview tool in Appendix A. Everyone in this book volunteered to share their lives. I recruited volunteers primarily online through Facebook, Reddit, Instagram, and other sources. Additionally, many people who were interviewed recruited their friends to be part of the book. As a result, the portraits reflect a large range of ages, genders, sex, marital status, cultures, and more.

After each interview, I transcribed what they said and did my best to create a portrait of their life. I intentionally tried to use direct quotes to allow each person to tell their own story in their own words. What that means is you will find a variety of voices in this book, and some may touch on tough topics or use what some consider inappropriate language. I intentionally chose not to censor anyone. This is your only trigger warning, as you may find quotes in here about real life, including death, sex, loss, and other difficult topics.

I look at my work in this book as a narrator or guide, with each portrait having its own hero. My goal was to allow each portrait to tell its own story and to pick out teachable moments to help you learn about Childfree Wealth, Life, and Finances. You will see some themes that became obvious throughout. Here are a few that might help you to gain context:

- **The reasons for being Childfree are as varied as the people themselves.** There are themes around why people choose to be Childfree (medical, financial, social, environmental, and others), and they are all valid. However, what was most surprising to me was the number of people who commented that they did not realize until later in their life that there was even a choice to be Childfree.

- **There are very few or no regrets from people being Childfree.** There is a clear theme that most people have no regrets about their choice to be Childfree. There are some fears for the future, but those are not regrets.

- **Being Childfree does not automatically make you rich.** What you will find in the portraits is that there are people who are barely making ends meet and others who are financially independent. I did find that Childfree people tend to have less debt than the average American. The way I look at it is that if you are Childfree and barely keeping your head above water, you would drown if you had a child.

- **There is a relationship between growing up poor and in poverty and being Childfree.** Unfortunately, I don't have enough data to determine if this is a correlation or causation relationship. Still, you will find that many of the portraits discuss growing up poor, in poverty, or lower class (their words).

- **COVID-19 had an impact.** This research was completed in February 2022. We had just been through two years of COVID-19 and shutdowns. Depending on when you read this, that may not seem like a big deal, but it was for many at the time.

- **Childfree Financial Independence is simple.** Most of those who achieved financial independence did two things: 1. They got out of debt (and stayed out), and 2. They maxed out their retirement plans. It is a rather boring and simple equation, but it seems to have worked for many.

- **Childfree people choose not to follow the LifeScript™.** While there isn't a formal written LifeScript™, you will see this term frequently in the Childfree community. It is a bit tongue in cheek, but represents all of the normal expected life choices, such as having a child.

- **Childfree people may prefer FILE over FIRE.** The FIRE (Financial Independence, Retire Early) movement is popular online. However, many Childfree people seem to be more interested in what I call FILE (Financial Independence, Live Early). If FIRE is an on/off switch for work, FILE is a dimmer switch (and reflects doing what you want for work or running a small business). For more on FILE versus FIRE, check out Appendix B.

- **The Gardener and the Rose may work for many.** My wife and I embrace the Gardener and the Rose approach. It allows one person to bloom (the Rose) while the other provides support (the Gardener). Childfree couples have more flexibility in their careers and may be able to embrace this approach. Remember that the Gardener and the Rose work best with planned "turns" or "swaps" between roles over time. For more, check out Appendix C.

- **Childfree Wealth reflects the ability to have the Time, Money, and Freedom to achieve your goals and dreams.** While each person might have put those in a different order, the bottom line is that being Childfree allows you all three.

How to Read This Book

My intent is not for you to read this book cover to cover. Each portrait is a stand-alone story. The result is that you may see some repetition in the themes (particularly in the notes from me), but that is intentional. I wanted you to be able to pick up this book, read one portrait and then take the time to reflect on it. Some portraits will hit you hard, and others you may not be able to connect with. That is okay.

One of my struggles was to decide the order of the portraits. I played with sorting them by age, income, life stage, and more. In the end, I decided to use alphabetical order by name. People choose to use their own name or a pseudonym, so even that may be a bit random. If you don't like the order I presented the portraits in, visit the table of contents, and you can pick a portrait based on the topic.

You will see that some topics (such as "A Portrait of Freedom") are duplicated. This is because I allowed each participant to weigh in on what to call their life a portrait of, and freedom was a common topic. That does not mean that the portraits are the same. They just have a similar theme in the eyes of the participant. We all have different definitions of freedom (and other terms), so each perspective is helpful.

I encourage you to do some active reflection on each story. What can you learn from it? What emotions does the story bring up in you? How does it support (or challenge) your own choices? Do they have goals or dreams that you share? How do you need to change your life to live your best Childfree life?

I also encourage you to discuss the portraits with friends and family. Share the book and the stories with others. It may help you to have a great discussion with others if you can center it around a portrait. For example, when I shared "Carly: A Portrait of Struggle" online, there were great discussions about income inequality, being Childfree, and supporting each other.

Try not to judge. Everyone in this book has had a different life than you. They have made different choices and will continue to make different choices than you would. Each choice is not better or worse, but just different. While they may have followed a different path than you, I genuinely believe that each portrait can help you learn something.

A note on definitions: For this book, I defined Childfree as "Not having children and not planning on having children." This is my definition, and yours might be different. Gatekeeping was not my intent, but it's important to have a definition for research purposes. You will see that some portraits stretch and challenge this definition, which is okay.

A Shameless Plug

This book is the first of two focusing on Childfree Wealth. I now have data from over 300 Childfree people about their life, wealth, and finances. The second book, Childfree Wealth, will focus on lived experiences and advice for you to improve your own life, wealth, and finances. It is scheduled to be released in Fall 2022, so keep your eye out for it.

I am also an Advice-Only, Fee-Only, Fiduciary CERTIFIED FINANCIAL PLANNER® and Childfree Wealth Specialist. That means that I help people achieve their dreams and improve their lives and finances. At the time of publication, I am the only CFP® professional specializing in helping Childfree individuals. You can learn more about my company, Live, Learn, Plan and Childfree Wealth, and about how I might be able to help you at https:// childfreewealth.com. I would love to hear from you, and I can also be reached via email at coachdrjay@gmail.com.

1

ALISON – A PORTRAIT OF FREEDOM

Alison
22, Female, Single, Missouri
Bachelor's in Creative Writing
Semi Truck Driver

Alison was on the road in Illinois headed to Texas when I spoke to her. She loves what she is doing, but her dream is to marry her current boyfriend and be a "lady of leisure." She has been to seven countries already and wants to keep traveling and learning. She has a list of goals a page long, but the bottom line is to do "whatever else I feel will make me happy."

So why did Alison choose to be Childfree?:

"There wasn't a reason behind it. It was just more from growing up. It wasn't very fun to be with children, even though I was a child as well. I kind of watched my aunt, who was young enough to be my older sister, grow up and go through high school. Then, she got pregnant at like 24, or 25. She turned from a really fun, really cool person that would take you to monster truck rallies and all that fun stuff like that to a stay-at-home. She was a mom who took care of three kids and was bored all the time. Then my summers turned into, instead of going out to like tractor pulls and fairs and stuff with my aunt to just like taking care of the kids. It wasn't, like, awful, but it just wasn't very appealing. I guess that would be like the main thing."

Her long-term boyfriend is also good with being Childfree. Was being Childfree part of the dating process?:

"Yeah. That's one of the first things they bring up. If they want kids, I just don't see them anymore. The funniest part is that during the dating process, I would be all like, oh, so how many kids do you want? You know, just kind of like poke the bear. So that way they answer me, like, oh, I don't want any or whatever. The answers from guys were crazy. I had a few guys that go: I want six to eight kids. I want 12 kids, and they're making like $25 an hour. So that was another thing. It was just like men just don't understand, like the consequence that having a child brings upon women and our bodies and the monetary expense of it all. It was just kind of crazy. What a lot of guys would want and expect from a woman was also just a massive turn-off. They were just like, my dad worked four jobs, and my mom stayed at home taking care of 12 kids. And I'm like, no, no, no."

So did her current boyfriend's answer that he did not want kids to push him to the top of the list?:

"No, he wasn't the only guy I had found that didn't want kids. I went to college for creative writing. A lot of the people that I was in there with didn't want kids and had no plans of having them. If they did want kids, it was a very far-off thing. Like, you know, after their careers had been established and they bought a house settled down somewhere like in their thirties. So, it was just kind of easy to find other childfree people, especially in college.

But it was different when I was in college, like working food stuff and retail. I was a salesman. I worked at Popeyes. A lot of the people there get paid minimum wage and have a lot of kids. So that's something that I've noticed a lot."

How did Alison go from creative writing to truck driving?:

"Well, the money truck driving makes me is quite good. I make about $1,000 a week, which is great. But like all of the internships that I was finding after college were trash. They were like, oh, we'll pay you nothing. And you get to bring us coffee. So I was like, never mind.

So, I was like, I'll just get a job that lets me travel. I have a journal that I'm writing about all my experiences in trucking and traveling. I do try to make time to stop at really cool places and check them out. I really like roller coasters. There are a lot of amusement parks. They even have a special place to park there. It's enjoyable."

Does Alison plan on sticking with trucking for life?:

"Funnily enough, I know people don't like this answer, but my long-term plan is just to be a stay-at-home wife."

How does she plan on getting to that life?:

"Well, my boyfriend, he's going to get a job that pays very well, better than mine, like three times. And I get paid $1,000 a week. That's not bad. That's not great either, though. But yeah, it should be fine.

I don't like to talk about it because it makes me nervous when I talk about it. I feel like a lot of people that we know make a lot of money, but they're also disabled in a way. So, all of their money goes towards medical bills. So, he's nervous that even though it might work financially, there are other considerations. We both are healthy people, for the most part. We don't engage in anything problematic. We're not drinkers or smokers. We eat vegetables. We're active."

The way Alison grew up may have shaped her relationship with finances:

"I grew up really poor. So like, it's just been like a high that I have money now. I have new shoes instead of wearing clothes from elementary school, which I still have. It's hard to break old habits. It feels weird, but when I got money like I just started spending money on more experience-based things."

What does Alison see as the biggest benefit of being Childfree?:

"The freedom of it. I like being able to have this job and travel and not have to worry about diapers. I used to babysit, but I only like really smart kids who can speak a couple of languages. I could speak Spanish, and the kids could speak English, Spanish, French, Hungarian or Bulgarian, or whatever their dad was. They were so smart, and I enjoyed seeing them because they were so smart and were polite. But that kind of child is probably not the kind of child that I would ever have."

Alison is looking forward to marrying her boyfriend. However, they aren't ready yet as they have both a marriage and engagement checklist:

"It feels like there's no rush. I take marriage very seriously. I don't like just rushing to get married because something might happen. My boyfriend and I make the joke that we're already both fat, so all we got to do is just grow old together.

We have a checklist of things that we want to have done. Like we want to credit scores that are 725 and be debt-free. He wants to have already gone to the academy and have placement. I know checklists aren't perfect, but we have things that we want to do before we get married and before we even get engaged."

Getting out of debt is a great goal. In my research, I've found that getting out of debt (and staying out) is the first step to financial independence. Childfree people who have achieved FIRE (Financial Independence, Retire Early) or FILE (Financial Independence, Live Early) did two things: 1. They got out of debt (and stayed out), and 2. They maxed out their retirement accounts. It is that simple.

Having a high FICO score does not mean you are in better financial condition, so why is it a goal for Alison?:

"Just because we would want to, like, either get an apartment together or get a house together. I recently went apartment hunting, and my credit score was a big factor in whether or not I got a nice apartment and how much it costs. So I just don't want to have a crappy apartment."

Alison seems to have a checklist and reason for everything. Does she have a financial plan?:

"I wouldn't call it a financial plan. I did start a budget. I'm not sure how much I'm going to stick to the plan just because it's relatively new, but yeah. I'm going to try to max out my Roth IRA this year and then try to get at least half of my debt paid off this year."

A financial plan does not have to be complex. Getting on a budget, maxing out her Roth IRA, and paying off half of her debt sounds like a great plan right now for Alison.

What are her plans for long-term care?:

"I liked the idea of living in a retirement community. He doesn't like the idea. I used to be a maid, and I got to come in on some of those ladies who lived there and their own, like, little retirement apartments. And they took a drink in their hand and just talked to all their friends, and it just seemed like a really good time. I would prefer that. You get a little house in a little retirement community. Like my great grandparents have that plan where they, like, have a little house and they have a little dog. There's a golf course nearby, and they can just cart to it. It just seems like a great, awesome place just to get old, have friends you see, and you can just cart around all the places you need to go. But you know, like if there was a medical emergency, like, you know, like you got the community there."

I've heard lots of variations of the retirement community for Childfree people. Some plan to have a community for single Childfree women, while others are more open, like Alison.

The question is, who will win the battle of where they are, Alison or her boyfriend?:

"I'm probably going to win."

It is also common for Childfree individuals to be expected to care for their elderly family members and others. So who is counting on Alison to take care of them?:

"My parents want me to take care of them, but we are not that close. So, it's kind of awkward. My sister likes to joke about the idea that I'm going to take care of her kids whenever she's in her thirties and whatever. And I'm like, you can't do that if I live cross country. I think my parents have finally realized that my sister and I are serious about not taking care of them just because they haven't been very nice people to us."

In the end, is Alison happy with her Childfree life?:

"I love my life. I have a fantastic job that lets me travel all over the U.S., Canada, and Mexico. I make a lot of money which means I can afford a luxury apartment by myself and whatever other luxuries I want, like biweekly massages and monthly facials, regular trips to the salon, nice clothes, nice furniture, a reliable car, expensive skincare, and several vacations. I get 52 days off a year, not including PTO or sick pay. The only way my life would be better is if I get to marry my boyfriend, the love of my life and best friend, retire from the workforce, and then focus 100% on my hobbies as a Lady of Leisure. I'm okay not rushing through this part of my life, however. I like having my own home and getting paid to be randomly sent around North America delivering goods. I am enjoying my early twenties and enjoying being a single (tax-wise), childless woman. I know life will change when I get married, but I'm lucky as I've found a good, generous, kind, caring, handsome, and thoughtful man to spend the rest of my life with who will only continue to add happiness and joy to my life. There's no rush to be married, either, which I like. I enjoy planning things, and my boyfriend knows this, and so we came up with large milestones we both want to hit before we tie the knot, which just makes me all the more excited to both marry him and continue living my best life."

2

AMELIA AND MATT – A PORTRAIT OF FREEDOM

Amelia
29, Female, Married, Colorado
Bachelor's in Sustainable Business
Sustainability Manager

Matt
33, Male, Married, Colorado
Automation Design

Amelia and Matt have been married for nine years and are living their best lives with a freedom that most would envy. Amelia works as a sustainability manager for a pet supplement company while Matt runs his own business in automation design. Matt also serves our country in the Air National Guard. They live with no debt, in a paid-for house with their dog and cat. They recently moved from Michigan to Colorado and have made sustainability and zero waste a large part of their life. Being Childfree is just part of their life, and as they shared:

"I think we were just, we never felt necessarily the drive to be parents. Like that was never like a goal or an ambition."

While Amelia and Matt never really wanted kids, they did consider adopting. Amelia shared:

"From the time I was little, I was in like middle school, and I was like, I am never birthing a child. I want to adopt. I was all about it. I wanted to adopt. And then we decided to be host parents for foreign exchange students."

Matt was on board:

"I was open to adoption just from an empathetic point of, like, these kids need homes. So sure, I could do that. But I did not want to be a dad, which creates a lot of problems. So we ended up hosting foreign exchange students."

Matt and Amelia suggest hosting foreign exchange students as a chance to "try out" having kids. Unfortunately, their experience did not go well. Amelia shared:

"We gave it a solid go, and we're really bad at it. Three of them left before their year was up because they hated living with us so much."

Matt continued:

"We liked her. We didn't like being parents. We didn't like having rules. We just did not like being parents. That was not fun. At that point, we were like, all right, this is a real clear indicator that we could just not have kids, and that'd be great."

So, do they have any thoughts about fostering now?

"No, I think the only instance that we've talked about of ever having kids is if something traumatic happened. For example, if my brother and sisters died and my nieces and nephews needed help, we would take them. We would take care of them. So, it's almost unrealistic that that would happen. We said we would be willing, but I think they know us."

When I asked what they think the most significant benefit of being Childfree is, Matt was quick to say it is Freedom:

"I think it's freedom for me. Freedom, autonomy. It's on a macro level, like this evening. If I want to go do a thing, I can just go and do a thing. It doesn't matter what the thing is. As long as I'm in good health, I can do anything. It doesn't matter. Same with financial freedom. If we want to ruin our financial trajectory for our future, that's fine. It doesn't affect our kids and doesn't affect anyone except the two of us. We don't even have the responsibility for somebody else to raise them. So, across the board, it is freedom."

They don't have any regrets about being Childfree and even see it as a way to prevent regrets, as Amelia explained:

"Growing up, I was an only child. My mom was a single parent. She was a good mom, and she loved me very much, but she also made it very clear that my birth kind of ruined her the trajectory that she had planned for herself. She didn't get to have the career she wanted or do the traveling that she wanted or do anything. So, I think that solidified it for me. I mean, you might have a kid and regret it too. That sounds a whole lot worse."

Amelia and Matt are happy with their life and living what I call the FILE lifestyle. If FIRE (Financial Independence, Retire Early) is an on/off switch for work, FILE (Financial Independence, Live Early) is a dimmer switch. It means doing the work you enjoy at a pace you enjoy. For Matt, that includes running his own small business. For Amelia, it means working a job that she wouldn't quit, even if she had more money than she knew what to do with:

> "I enjoy my job. My career is something that I've been passionate about since I was young. I love sustainability. I love that I get to go to work every day, and it sounds dumb, but I feel like I'm impacting the world. It's fantastic. I'm trying to leave our planet, if not in a better place, make it less bad than it could be."

They are far enough on the path to financial independence that they can make different decisions, as Matt explained:

> "We're on a trajectory towards financial independence, way sooner than expected. So, we've been thinking about reaching financial independence. We've been living our life that way. Amelia has taken job opportunities that she's had a passion for. We up and moved to Colorado when Amelia lost her last job. I just quit my job and said, screw it, I'm moving. I just opened a company. If it fails, it fails. If it goes great, it goes great... I think Amelia is passionate about sustainability and the stuff that she impacts on the grand scale. For me, I love a lot of design work. I just love designing things and being creative."

Besides a bit more travel and volunteering at a dog rescue in Spain, Amelia and Matt are living their ideal life. COVID-19 has cramped some of their travel plans, but they have a big trip planned to Mexico with a group of friends soon. That trip was scheduled for a while. It was a bit of a celebration and reconnection since Matt had just returned from his second deployment with the Air National Guard. They don't need an excuse to travel, however. It is just part of their life and something they can do because they are Childfree:

> "I think travel is tough to do when you have kids. Yeah, they say it's possible. I'm in a few travel groups on Facebook, and there's a

women's travel group. In the group, all the time, there's somebody who says: I just got pregnant and I'm not going to be able to travel anymore. People try to say that you still can travel; you just do it differently. Then they, like, disappear and you never see them again, and that's just how it goes. It's just so much easier to travel without kids because you can be more reckless too. When we went to Colombia, everybody was like, you are going to die. You're just going to get murdered. That is not how it went. Colombia was lovely. But if you had a kid that you were responsible for, you wouldn't bring your child to the rainforest."

Travel is a widespread hobby in the Childfree population. For Matt and Amelia, travel ranges from road trips staying in hostels and Airbnb to an all-inclusive resort. They love interacting with friends, families, and strangers. As Matt shared:

> "We love people. We absolutely love people, but we don't like the idea of creating people. We love strangers. We're the kind of people that love to travel, meet strangers and just chat for hours and have drinks."

They can travel and live their best lives because they have the freedom and the finances to do it. It wasn't that they were born with money, far from it. As Matt shared:

> "We both grew up in trailers, dirt poor."

Amelia credits growing up in this environment as part of the reason they are so driven:

> "We grew up in a really small, really poor town in Northern Michigan. There was a lot of poverty, a lot of drugs, and it's not a great place to be, but we got out. So that's good. I think what makes us so driven is because that's where we came from. We grew up watching our parents struggle."

Matt shared about his life growing up:

"I heard a lot growing up that you guys are expensive, you guys cost this, you guys are a drain. We don't have any money. My parents are divorced, and my dad made like $70,000 or $80,000 a year, which would be considered well off, but we lived paycheck to paycheck at best. He was in mountains of debt. He had six kids he was feeding. He was terrible with money to start. So there was a lot of that growing up where you saw irresponsibility. I mean, you either have role models, or you have people that you don't want to be like, right? So, he was an example of somebody financially that I didn't want to be. Then my parents, on the other side, my mom and stepdad, had no money. They weren't necessarily great with their money, but they started getting a little bit better. You could see the impact of your financial decisions, and I liked that a lot better. With my dad and as far as having kids plays into finances, it looked like there was no win. It was never helpful in any way."

Growing up poor, in poverty, or lower class is a recurring theme in my research on the Childfree lifestyle. I don't know if it is a correlation or causation relationship, but it is common enough to be a trend. The challenge with poverty is that it can be tough to get out of. Matt and Amelia have worked hard, graduated college, and now are in a great financial situation early in their lives. They are goal-driven people. The challenge comes once you have achieved your goals, as Amelia shares:

"I think we're at an exciting spot right now. Matthew just got home from deployment last week. My goals were to graduate high school, and I wanted to graduate college. The minute I graduated college, I wanted to find full-time work in my field, which frankly was not the easiest thing to do and took a few years. And by the time I got full-time work in my field, I was like, just kidding. I don't like Michigan. I want to move to Colorado. And that took quite a few years. And then, by the time I came out here, we knew he was going to be leaving in a couple of months. So, that was looming. And then he left, and I was like, okay, I just have to get through this. He's got to come back home...

The point is that now we're finally at a point where the next goal is retirement, which is about ten years away. I'm excited about it. But for the first time it feels, it doesn't feel like life is going to start. This week has been the first week where I still have financial goals and want to retire, but it's not something that I'm chasing hard. If retirement gets pushed out a couple of years, I don't care. My goals are more around having meaningful friendships and developing those relationships. Also, traveling more and being a well-connected member of my community that can give back and be a good resource to people I mentor. They're not really like, oh yeah, I need to do X."

Matt sees the goal of FIRE as easy and just a matter of going through the steps:

"I mean, we're both goal-oriented, and we have met a lot of our goals. A lot of the FIRE steps are very achievable, straightforward goals. Paying your house off is like literally just putting money in, and the house is paid off. Right? It is just a lot of achievable goals. I think we've achieved a lot of the goals we've set for ourselves up to this point. We are to a point where our goals now are much loftier. Like a goal of retiring early, we're going to do that. We're hitting milestones and stuff to do that."

So, what financial plan did they follow to get there? As Amelia says:

"I've got a spreadsheet."

As Matt explains:

"We're Excel nerds."

It isn't about following a strict spending plan for them but tracking their progress, retirement accounts, and the like. The key to them is that they are completely debt-free, including their mortgage. While growing up, the most significant advice they got was to keep their credit score up. It may have been the example from their families that convinced them to get rid of debt altogether:

"I think it was for me at least a hundred percent how I grew up. My mom was always in so much debt, and everything was on credit cards and racking up a ton of interest. I know it stressed her out a bunch, and it just made me nervous, and it was not how I wanted to live my life. So we made sure not to get into debt. We did have student loans. We had a car loan once, and we had a mortgage for a few years. Debt just made me uncomfortable. I understand that it's not always the most financially smart thing to pay off debt. I mean, our mortgage was like 3% interest, and it's not necessarily the smartest financial move to pay it off. I know that, but it was just like the psychological relief of not being in debt was important to us."

Amelia's story is familiar. The vast majority of Childfree people I have talked to who achieved FIRE (or FILE) did two things: they paid off all of their debt and maxed out their retirement accounts. To Matt's point, it isn't complex. It is just ticking off tasks. Pay consumer debt first, then invest in retirement and pay off your house. Paying off all of their debt was just another tool, like being Childfree, that gives Matt and Amelia freedom to live their best life as she shared:

"It worked out for us. When COVID hit, I lost my job. The entire sustainability department at my company was eliminated. Because we didn't have any debt at all, it was fine. Like, okay, I lost my job. Cool. And I looked at Matt and said we're going to move. I lost my job, made him quit his. We moved across the country. Because we owned our home outright, we had options. We wouldn't have been able to qualify for a mortgage as neither of us had income at that point. But because we own our home, we could sell it and take that money to buy our home here. We would never have been able to make that move if we had a mortgage. There was way more freedom to make a move when the opportunity presented itself. So, it was the right choice for us."

3

AURORA – A PORTRAIT OF GETTING STARTED

Aurora
26 years old, Single, Female, Texas
College Courses in Information Technology
Implementation Analyst

A urora is 26 and has recently chosen to be Childfree. She is working through what that means to her as she finds her place in the world. Her passions include sewing, crochet, gaming, baking, cooking, and alone time. Her most significant influence in choosing to be Childfree was watching her mom struggle, and it became a concrete choice to her at 25:

"It became concrete when I had a pregnancy scare at 25. I've calmed down from that, and it's like, in the moment of thinking I was pregnant, I realized I don't have a support system. I don't make enough money. I don't have a decent co-parenting partner because he was, like, a deadbeat. Then I was, like, there was a way for me not to have to experience this fear again, and it's just being Childfree. My heritage and my upbringing are African-American. So, most of the time, from a place of not addressing trauma, we fall into this cycle of, oh, I'm just living to pay bills. I broke that mindset in December of 2021 [approximately four months before the interview]. Now I'm starting to figure out what I want to do and where I would like to go and my career and stuff like that. And I don't want just to mess all that up when I'm just getting started."

What does Aurora see as the biggest benefit of being Childfree?:

"For me, it gives me my time. I get time back because for a while in my life, for like four years, I was working the third shift. Now that I've started my career, my first step is a day shift job. The switch from overnight to daytime is like night and day. I have so much time that I don't know what to do with the time. I'm working on a decent productivity schedule because I'm going to school in April. I'm working on getting some IT certifications and teaching myself coding. So I just basically get to do whatever. And I get to take my time doing it. I'm not under any type of stress unless I give myself a deadline."

Does Aurora have regrets about her choice to be Childfree?:

"Heck no, not yet."

Aurora is looking into sterilization but faces some challenges:

"I'm looking into sterilization, but as a bigger woman, it's more of a push for me. The first doctor I've tried is pushing me to get weight loss before I have the surgery. I was advised by the wonderful support group of women that exist in this world just to try and get a different doctor. The issue with birth control is that it causes weight gain. So how are you going to lose weight on something that causes weight gain? And I don't want to come off because I don't want to be at risk."

Aurora's experience is relatively standard. There are all types of stories of women having difficulty getting sterilized for various reasons. That is why the Childfree community maintains a list of "friendly" doctors. It's sad that we have to keep a list, but good that we know who supports our community.

Does Aurora have a financial plan at this point?:

"I just know that if there's something I want, I will sacrifice and save up for it. If I don't want anything, I just focus more on saving... The first plan is an emergency fund. I depleted it last year when I dealt with some unexpected changes. So I have to rebuild it, and then I'm saving up for a trip to New York and car repairs. I have opened two investment accounts. Nothing's written down. I just came up with numbers to try to automate. I like to automate my finances as much as possible."

Aurora had shared that she was in debt (including auto and student loans which are very common), but getting out of debt wasn't mentioned as part of her financial plan. Why?:

"I didn't write the debt part down. That's not written down now because I chip away at it like you're making a sculpture, but I don't have a definite plan to attack it. I never have because that's the thing that caused me stress. I didn't figure out until the summer of last year that creating a definite plan to attack it causes me stress. So instead, I'm just focusing on, okay, we're going to attack this one this year, and then next year, we're going to attack this one."

Debt is stressful to most people. The challenge is that debt is stealing from your future. In most cases, you will be better off paying off your debt before investing. Paying off your debt is effectively a risk-free, guaranteed return. The problem is that debt can be overwhelming. When you are in $10K of debt, adding another $500 of debt for many people feels no different. Aurora is focusing on investments because the debt causes her stress. Her goal is to have $2 million to retire.

What advice would Aurora give to others who are just getting started?:

"Find friends and ask questions. Find friends, try to have constant reminders within yourself about why you want to be Childfree. So for me, subconsciously, I've established friendships with multiple moms. So, I continually have reminders that I don't want to deal with this. There have been times when I'm just lying in bed and lonely right now. I wish I had somebody that I could, like, talk to. I know I can't talk to them. They're always busy doing something. I've managed to have one Childfree friend. I am still looking for other friends, and I prefer them to be single.

Find friends, ask questions and join online Facebook groups. They are the safest place that I've found so far. So join the Facebook groups and, if possible, use Meetup.com to find people near you, other groups, or interests that you want to explore. So that way you can explore with other people. And you'll never know who in those groups is also going to be Childfree and just seeking the same thing. So you're thinking simple friendship."

I asked Aurora what the most significant benefit of the Facebook groups is:

"Safety, especially like non-biased emotional safety. That is brand new to me. That's something I've never been given before. I've never had people tell me all the time: you can come to talk to me. So, to just make a Facebook post and have, like, so many kind words and advice given back to me, that was, that was brand-new and made me cry."

4

AUTUMN – A PORTRAIT OF TOO MANY CHOICES

Autumn
28, Non-binary, Married, Oklahoma
Associate's Degree in Business
Changing Careers

A utumn is 28 and has been married for almost a decade. Autumn is an actress, audiobook recorder, and writer. She hopes one day to publish her own book. As she says:

"I have two fur kids and live in the most boring state in the country: Oklahoma."

Right now, with the support of her husband, she is searching to find herself and the right career but may have too many choices available.

Why did Autumn decide to be Childfree?:

"I'm the oldest of four to a single mother. She struggled a lot when I was younger. I remember digging through the couch for change so she could get gas. Then, one night when my brother was a newborn (we were 13 years apart), I saw her struggle, which opened my eyes to the reality of parenthood. I learned early on that kids are never in my future ever. No matter whether it's adopting or naturally or any of that shit. They're expensive. They're loud. They will keep coming back home. Even whenever you kick them out, they move back because they need to due to the economy, which is fantastic.

I have an awful relationship with my family. I am the black sheep. I am the one who is the complete opposite of everything they are. So I've gotten to experience what it's like to be disowned. I've gotten to experience what it's like to be an unwanted child, as it were. So that opened my eyes to like, just because you're blood doesn't mean shit.

Babies are really, really annoying, and I am scared to death of pregnancy. I have seen what it does, the human body. And I'm just like, no, no, thank you. That is terrifying. And they don't even tell you all that could happen with pregnancy because they know that nine times out of ten, we won't have them because it's insane.

The state of the world is also a really good reason not to have kids: climate change and the whole nine yards. I don't understand how people are still popping out kids in the 2020s. It's just bizarre."

What does Autumn see as the biggest benefit of being Childfree?:

"Being able to change my mind about what I want to do with my life, how I want to live it. I'm still figuring my own life out. I'm 28, and I still feel young. I don't know what I want in life, and that's okay because I don't have people depending on me. Like, I can quit a job that I don't like. I can quit a career that I hate. I'm not reliant on that money for someone else whom you can't get rid of.

I only recently decided to be an author, and I've always wanted to be an actress. I've always wanted to be like a travel blogger, but you can't do all those things if you have kids. My career choices are so much better if I'm Childfree."

Does Autumn have any regrets about her choice to be Childfree?:

"Hell no, no. None. Zero nada."

Autumn is at a crossroads in her life. She is trying to figure out what is next. Fortunately, her husband makes enough to make ends meet while she finds her passion. I call this approach "the Gardener and the Rose." Each person takes a turn being the Rose and growing, while the other provides support (Gardening). Right now, it is Autumn's turn to be the Rose:

> "I want a career, not just a job; you know what I mean? I'm still trying to pay for school, despite the fact that we have debt. We have debt coming out of our eyeballs.
>
> I used to work from home as a customer service representative, and then I would also schedule people for COVID vaccinations. Then they stopped doing that and sent us to another company. That company decided to let some of us go, and I was one of the few that were let go. And ever since then, I've pursued other companies, but I'm just really burnt out on that. I'm burnt out on customer service. I'm burnt out on just normal jobs. You know what I mean?"

In each interview, I use a series of questions by George Kinder. The three questions ask about what you would do if you were financially secure, or if you only had five or 10 years to live, or 24 hours to live. The intent is to help people reflect on what matters to them in life. After those questions, I ask: Is there anything you need to be doing differently now?:

> "Yeah. Thanks for another existential crisis. I need to work more on my books. I need to work on a career. I need to reconnect with my fam, if that's even possible. Probably not hang out with my friends who are across the pond. And I might be social more. I kinda noticed like COVID-19 kind of screwed over my socialness. I'm pretty sure it made me agoraphobic, not going to lie."

I think many of us may have a bit of agoraphobia after COVID-19.

So what is holding Autumn back from achieving her dreams?:

"Money, namely money and location. I'm currently in a location where, as I describe it, where dreams die. I'm in the Midwest, and there's not a whole lot of theatre community here, or really most of the arts aren't here. We're mainly like agriculture, nothing I give a fuck about.

We're trying to move, but mostly we ended up moving from town to town to city within Oklahoma because it's cheap. The very thought of moving to Oregon right now, or California, or anywhere where there are opportunities available, is tough. Have you seen the bread prices? And the prices of anything now? On what we make now, we could never afford it."

After diving in a bit more, it became apparent that the location may be even more important than the right career for Autumn. Is her husband on the same page?:

"Oh yeah, he knows. I drive him crazy. I have what we call a continual existential crisis. I get really depressed. I've gotten really depressed every year of this pandemic, to say the least. I go through periods of stir craziness. I go through times of existential dread. I go through times of wanting to just, you know, burn my life down and start over again. Like I go through that a lot. He's used to it by now, but I do drive him crazy because I had ambition, but with ambition and drive, it's the life circumstances that tend to kick you in the ass.

I love him to death, but if I were to die, I have no, like, you know, monetary value to him. Most artists don't become valued until they're dead, which is really, really, really sad.

Ever since he picked up this job and he told me to pursue my own dreams, I've kind of, like, been well, what about your own dreams? Like, do you have ambition outside of just, you know, driving? You know, like I remember whenever you wanted to go to Julliard. I remember when you wanted to play an instrument in an orchestra. Those things can still happen, and we've done it before. Just not now. We are still a work in progress."

The challenge of being the Rose (in the Gardener and the Rose) is that it can be hard to focus on yourself and be selfish (as you should be). Autumn seems to be bouncing between wanting to live her best life, guilt, and a never-ending cycle of reflection. I asked her if guilt was holding her back from really going for what she wanted? Her answer:

"Definitely. Yes."

At the core of the Gardener and the Rose is an agreement that a couple will take turns in each role. So no one is stuck as either the Gardener or the Rose for life. It might help Autumn if she set this type of agreement with her husband. My wife and I have that arrangement. We recently moved 1,200 miles so that she could have her dream job (she is the Rose now). We've agreed that when I hit 59, I'm the Rose (and we will be boating the world, which is what I want to do as the Rose).

What does Childfree Wealth mean to Autumn?:

"No worries. Like honestly, you see parents worrying about every-thing, right? I have to worry about where my income is going with us. The wealth is in the freedom. I don't have to take my kids to ballet practice. In fact, I don't even have to take them [her two dogs] to the dog park all that often because they often forget if they've gone to the dog park that week. And I can decide whether we want to go or not. Is the weather too cold? If so, we ain't going, we're going to snuggle on the couch, and they're fine with that. And in fact, they like watching 'Downton Abbey' with me, which is fantastic. They don't bark. They don't do anything but watch and snuggle.

We can have an abundant life. Like most parents rely on their kids to live out their dreams, but they were never fulfilled. But with us, we can live our dreams. If anything, you know, sometimes we hold ourselves back, but that's just us, you know, not our kids."

I was a bit surprised by Autumn's answer, as she had spent much of the interview explaining the worries she had for her life, career, location, and more. How does she square having no worries with the worries she listed?:

"Right? How do I explain this? Sometimes my brain just doesn't articulate. Well, we have money worries. We have worries about our future. We have worries about climate change and war. And if we're going to be able to fulfill our dreams before the world collapses. My worries are different from a parent's worry. I feel like a parent's worry, it's 10,000 times heavier than mine because they have to worry about literally everything about their kids, all day, every day, they don't get a break. They don't get to breathe for a second.

Me, I can turn off my brain and say, fuck it. I'm not worrying about the money today. Fuck it. I'm not worrying about my book today. Fuck it. I'm not worried about anything. I'm not even going to clean the house, and I can do that because I don't have little ones."

I hear Autumn. I get what she is saying. However, I would challenge her that no one's worries are more or less important than anyone else's. We all choose what is important to us and what we want to worry about. The challenge with being Childfree is that we may have too many options and get stuck in analysis paralysis. We can get stuck in our heads and not make progress.

Does Autumn have a set of goals for her life?

"Yes, I have an entire list, but the main one is to make an impact. I don't care what it is. Obviously, it's not going to be a child. That's not my legacy, but I want to make a mark on the world. Whether it be a book or a piece of work, or something within the community. I want to travel. I want to make all the friends I can 'cause life is certainly lonely without them. I want to fill the need for found family, which is a big one. I don't think a lot of people get it, especially if they've never been disowned. They don't understand the need for 'found family.' Also, the whole not worrying about money thing is it's up there, of course, but it doesn't matter how I get there. You know, like whether it be a book, which is like a one in a million chance, or with a steady job either, or it doesn't matter."

Autumn is not the first person to say they want to make a mark. Each person has a different measure of what that means, but I do not doubt that Autumn will make one. The big question is just how. She may be struggling with having too many choices, but I am sure she will achieve whatever she sets her mind to once she picks. What advice does she have for others?:

"For those doubting or constantly like on the fence? This Childfree life is the best life I've ever chosen. And I have no regrets. Just trust me on this."

5

BETTY – A PORTRAIT OF STARTING OVER

Betty
38, Female, Pansexual, New York
Master's in History
Digital Editor

Betty is starting over and finding her true self. She started her life working in museums and is now a digital editor. She has been married and divorced twice and is now enjoying her life with her three cats. She is polyamorous. Betty is Childfree, and like many of us, that has allowed her the flexibility to start over and live her life on her terms.

I start my interviews with the "hardest" question, "Introduce yourself as you would at a party or social gathering." While many interviewees struggle as they have forgotten what a social gathering was over the COVID-19 period, Betty's struggle is because she is in a time of transition:

"It is a hard question. Honestly, I don't know. I'm the kind of person that in the past would have defined myself more by my career, but I changed careers last year, and it's been a hard transition. So, I'm not sure how I would introduce myself now.

I'm a historian. I have two degrees in history. I spent 12 years working for nonprofit history, art, and STEM-focused museums. So that was kind of my identity for the longest time. I'm trying to get away from that a little bit. I switched careers to become a digital editor for an SEO marketing company. The work is fine. I don't find it difficult or challenging really in any way.

I'm trying to learn how to separate myself and my identity from my work. So in that regard, I would probably describe myself as a knowledge seeker. I listen to podcasts. I watch a lot of documentaries. I read a lot of nonfiction. I'm always seeking new information beyond that. I'm Childfree. I've been married and divorced twice. I have three cats. I live alone most of the time. I'm polyamorous, and I have a partner that is local and lives here part-time. He's over here a couple of days a week, but doesn't contribute financially to my life here really in any way, other than occasionally buy me dinner or something."

Betty's story is not "odd." Being Childfree allows us to stretch, learn, and reinvent ourselves. We aren't stuck to one area or job. Betty has moved 35 times in her life and three times in less than a year. Her hope now is to buy a house, work remotely for the rest of her life and settle down. She followed her passion and worked in some fantastic museums across the country. COVID-19 hit museums hard and pushed Betty towards making a change. Now it is on to the next phase of her life. All of the moving and flexibility would not have been possible if she had a kid and Betty decided to be Childfree at a young age:

"I was probably eight years old when I learned that my mother had her 'tubes tied' after she had my younger brother. When I found out that she could never have any more kids, I was like, oh, I want one of those. And that desire never really went away. Growing up and seeing what people go through with kids and being a kid in a less than ideal situation reinforced it. My parents got divorced, and I was never abused or neglected or anything, but we moved around all the time. And here I am as an adult repeating the same thing. We never had enough money. You know, we were never poor. We were never hungry. It was just always renting, always moving.

My parents were military. And one of the reasons why they got divorced was because they took on too much, too soon, too fast. They were 22 when they got married. I also got married the first time at 22, which was a massive mistake. Thankfully, I didn't have kids as they did. They split up because they had serious financial issues.

Everything that I saw about having kids just seemed like a big trap. There are enough traps in life, and the older I've gotten and the more of a feminist I've become, the more I've seen that it is a trap for women specifically. There are a lot of Childfree men out there. They'll be like, oh, she was trying to baby trap me. She's going to get my wallet. She might get your money, but she's not gonna get your whole life. If you're a woman and you become a mother, that all of a sudden has to be your whole life."

Betty shared that she is queer and polyamorous. So, I asked her, is it okay if her partners have kids?:

"Yes, actually my only partner right now for the last two years, since the pandemic, has a child, and actually, he's kind of like co-parent to my cats, which is weird."

I followed up on this to dive deeper. With single Childfree people, there is often a discussion on if they can date moms or dads. Most say no. Does it matter to Betty at all if her partners have kids?:

"No. I don't have any intention of cohabitating with anybody on any kind of full-time or traditional basis anymore. It doesn't matter to me at all. I push back against people who say, oh, you're dating somebody with kids, you're not Childfree. That's bullshit. I didn't give birth. I'm sterilized. Childfree, thank you. I don't contribute financially to anyone else's offspring. So, I'm not even supporting kids."

Betty is right that there is some gatekeeping in the Childfree community. For this book, I defined Childfree as "Don't have kids, not planning on having kids" (which would qualify Betty), but the definition of Childfree is fluid. Betty isn't planning on getting married again, which is part of the picture. I asked her if she would ever get married again:

"I don't think so. Honestly, I don't know. I think about how different my life would have to be. Then I think about the LAT movement (Living Apart Together)? I could see some sort of, probably not even like, legal marriage, like maybe like a commitment ceremony, and we still live separately. So, I may get married again, and maybe in a very nontraditional sense."

Does Betty have any regrets about her choice to be Childfree?:

"No, I don't regret not birthing or adopting children of my own. The older I get, the more I like kids. It's cool to meet people with kids because kids are funny. Honestly, babies and toddlers are boring to me, but once a kid can have a conversation with you, they're just fun. And they're funny. I even like teenagers. Teenagers are sort of unwittingly funny some of the time, which is just great. I've dated people that have had teenagers, and hanging out with their kids was fun."

For now, Betty is trying to find herself and her future. In each interview, I ask a series of hypothetical questions about what you would do if you had financial independence or if you had five or 10 years to live or only 24 hours left. After those questions, I asked Betty to reflect on what she should be doing differently now. She reflected that she should be making more money to live a happier life. So I followed up and asked her how making more money would make her happier?:

"I would be able to give myself a secure place to live. That would be great. That would take a load off my mind to be able to have savings. To replace my 13-year-old car when it no longer makes sense to keep fixing it. Thankfully it is a Volkswagen, and it is very hardy. I'd be able to travel more, to be able to, to meet more people, and kind of get out of my shell. It depends. It is the main thing that I've been thinking about lately."

The hard part is to achieve a balance between working more, making more, and being happy. If you are working more at a place that drains your joy, there isn't enough money out there to make you happy. So how is Betty planning on achieving the balance between making more and happiness?:

"I've been trying to start this part-time thing and sort of mentally preparing myself to kind of buckle down and work two jobs until I find something better. Right now, my full-time job is okay enough that it's not worth me quitting for just some other random job that pays the same. If I found a job that paid 50% more, I would quit. Since I've changed fields, I'm trying to get as much on my resume reflecting the new career field. With museum work, I was at the peak. I was at executive director level, and I took an executive director job as my last gig. And even in the midst of that, I had seven other museums wanting me to be their executive director. The museum I ended up going with was in New York, and it ended up being a bad fit for a number of reasons. I'm happy that it was at least in the same state."

Does Betty miss the museum work?:

"I miss some of the work. I don't miss the executive director stuff. That was shit. I miss being a curator, but the problem is it didn't pay enough. The public history field and museum field are so competitive. There are way more qualified people and overqualified people than there are ever going to be jobs. And I fought the rat race for 12 years, and I moved 5,000 miles for school and then for jobs in the field back and forth across the Eastern half of the United States, a couple of times. That sucked."

So then, what is Betty going to do?:

"I'm working as an editor, and there are all different kinds of editors. What I'm doing right now is more on the side of copy editing, which is fine. I'd love to be a developmental or content editor for educational materials. I've tried to get on a couple of times with different companies that make curriculum materials for schools, so far, no dice. At this point, I'm open to opportunities."

What Betty wants right now is stability. She has moved so much that she wants to set down roots and buy a house. She currently rents, and the place is drafty (she needs to cover the windows with plastic to keep out the cold), the stove is older than she is, and the landlord is largely absent. The challenge is that the current housing market is a bit crazy. My advice is to rent until she figures out her career, but she plans on working remotely (from home) for the rest of her life.

Starting over isn't new to Betty, as she shared:

"I keep starting over in a new life every couple of years."

The challenge is that at some point, that gets old. Betty is doing what she needs to do to find her best life. She sees social media posts online with people "flexing" and talking about their perfect Childfree life. That isn't her life, but she is still happy with her Childfree life:

"Some of us are just trying to get by and thank God we don't have children to worry about on top of everything else... I've made a lot of mistakes in my life, and I try not to have too many regrets, but in terms of things that make me go yes, past you, you did a fantastic job not having kids. Congratulations on not having kids."

6

CARLY – A PORTRAIT OF STRUGGLE

Carly
32, Female, Married, Colorado
Bachelor's in Business, working on a Master's
Part-Time IT Professional (while finishing school)

Carly, like many others in the United States, is struggling. Her husband is Bulgarian, and they moved back from Bulgaria to the U.S. at the end of February 2020. We all know that COVID-19 would reshape our world just days later, but the reality is that you couldn't pick a worse time to move and restart your life. Since that time, Carly and her husband have struggled to make ends meet while Carly went back to school for a bigger and brighter future. The one thing that makes it easier for them is that they are Childfree.

All of Carly's siblings have kids, and her husband's sibling is having his first. The result is that Carly and her husband are the last ones standing and the pressure to have kids is strong:

"We're going to make it. I'm just worried. The walls are closing in, and there's going to be so much pressure. Especially from his family, but we will make it. It'll just be irritating for a while."

Carly has been clear on her choice to be Childfree since she was about 22:

"I think when I was about 22, so like, almost a full decade ago. I was having a conversation with a friend who was around my age. She had already decided to be childfree, and it had never even occurred to me up until then that it was even a choice. I just thought, [having kids] is what you do. It's the life script. It's what's expected of you from your family and society. And I had some really good conversations with my friend about that. Everything she said resonated with me, like why she didn't want kids. It's like, wait a minute, I feel that myself. And some of these things that she was saying would be a good reason not to have a kid. So I started thinking, why do I need to sign myself up for this? It was a really quick transition from being in the back of my head; I'm going to probably have kids one day too; no, I'm not doing this. This is not for me."

Carly's husband was kind of ambivalent about having kids but was okay with being Childfree. They did discuss it early on, but no drawn-out debates; he was just cool with it. Carly sees the most significant benefit of being Childfree as not having responsibility for a child:

"I would say, not having that responsibility [of having kids] and not having all the stress that has come with a pandemic and like having a small child or kids in school. I have family that has gone through that with their kids, and I cannot imagine the levels of stress they went through. It was bad enough not having kids, especially in the beginning. I just kept thinking in the back of my mind, like, thank God, I don't have a child that I have to figure out how to protect from this whole crazy crisis [COVID] that's going on."

Carly only has one regret about being Childfree:

"The only time I regret anything is when I feel like members of the family get more attention. This is actually really petty of me, I'm sure. They get more attention when there's a pregnancy announcement. I've written articles that have been published. I've been in school, making great grades for almost a decade. Now I've been in and out of classes, and it's like, oh, whatever, she's doing that, that's fine. And when somebody is pregnant, oh my gosh, we have to make a huge deal about it. I mean, it's not enough that I would want to have a baby just for the attention, but it does irritate me. Especially the older I get. I'm like, why did I have to choose something that makes me feel so ostracized sometimes?"

Carly loves to travel. One day she would love to open a travel-related business. She was on that path at the beginning of 2020, but then COVID-19 hit. She is currently finishing her Master's degree and figures she will have to work some other job to get some stability before following her dreams. She has the passion and dreams to start a business, but it is overwhelming to think about now. Right now, Carly and her husband are just trying to make ends meet:

"Early on in the pandemic when we were kind of struggling. We did not have a couch. We didn't even have a real bed for a while. We had to sleep on an air mattress... I did have somebody ask me once: where does all your money go? Because you don't have kids [and must be rich]. I'm like, well, I have rent, I have a car. And these things are ridiculously expensive. Rent was horrific where we were. I couldn't even imagine having to have a two-bedroom. It was insane. But yeah, they were still, where's all your money? Like, I can show you my bank account."

Carly took a terrible job when they moved back to the U.S., and her husband's work was cut. He is a graphic designer and artist, and 2020 was a bad year. So I asked Carly if they have financial goals:

"Not anything sharply defined right now. It has kind of been like broader goals. The first one is, finding a job that is a certain percentage more than what I'm making now. Same thing for my husband. He's getting into some coding classes to hopefully, find some kind of work that can supplement [his artwork]."

Carly is passionate about travel but realistic. Her husband is passionate about his art. I asked her which is more important, having money or following your passions:

"That's hard because I feel like I need money to follow my passions. If I could follow my passions and survive, that would be fine. I think I would be fine with that as long as I loved what I did. But that's such a catch-22 for me right now. Not having money is why I'm not following my passions like this second. I would rather have some kind of job that allowed me to do what I loved. Even if it didn't pay an amazing amount of money, that would still be preferable for me."

Knowing their situation, it was a terrible question for me to ask, but it is a choice we all have to make each day. Do we follow our heart and passions or follow the dollars? Carly and her husband have no problem living in a small apartment or giving up nice things if it means they can follow their passions:

"We're perfectly happy with, like, a small space and modest things."

Carly and her husband are debating living in the U.S. or Bulgaria. Carly has family in the U.S., and he has family in Bulgaria. They did live in Bulgaria for a while and enjoyed it. Now it is just a question of what they want to do after Carly finishes school:

"We're kind of really starting to lean towards Bulgaria at this point for a lot of reasons. The health care system in this country has been a big problem for us. Even just the cost and the trouble to get insurance. And then the insurance is awful. You don't have these problems in Bulgaria. They have public health care. It's not quite as good as the public health care that the U.K. has, but it's close. It's leagues better than here. The cost of living is just getting out of control here, and wages aren't matching it. It is the same in Bulgaria to an extent, but you don't have this really drastic difference between the two. Wages are keeping up better with rising rent and food and that kind of thing. So we're thinking, you know, these financial goals we have, it might be easier to meet them if we're there. If we could work remote jobs, that would open up a lot more for both of us."

Carly and her husband are working through the mountain of paperwork to handle visas and citizenship for Bulgaria. They aren't alone. Living as an expatriate is becoming popular. There are some interesting tax and financial considerations, but it may make sense for Carly and her husband. They originally planned to live in the U.S. for a while so that her husband could see what it was like, and then decide where they wanted to live. They made a move just before COVID-19 hit:

"I think we were on one of the last flights that didn't have a mask mandate. There were no masks on flights because there was still like, oh, it's going to go away in a couple of weeks. And then we get here, and just everything is on fire. We were just like watching this dumpster fire unfold. It turned out that a global pandemic needed not to happen at the same time as everything we had planned. That's where the heart of the struggle stems from."

Being Childfree helped them get through the struggle, and if they had a kid, they might not have made it:

"The worst part of everything, which was that towards the end of 2020, before we had the vaccines and everything, a lot of stuff happened at once. Not just, you know, on a global level, but on personal levels, a lot of stuff was happening. My mental health took a hard hit. Like it was hit harder than I think it's ever been hit in my life. I don't think I could have taken care of a kid, even if I wanted to. I mean, I might've had to tell my husband, you know, take that kid away, or I might wind up hurting them. I was in some really dark places. I had no patience. I was snapping at people. I was getting maybe two or three hours of sleep at night because my insomnia was horrible during that period. I don't think I could have had a kid under my roof and expected it to end well during that period."

The combo of COVID-19 and dealing with family and bureaucracy in both countries have pushed Carly and her husband to the edge:

"It was hard with COVID and trying to deal with the bureaucracy on both sides. My husband was trying to establish residency here while I'm trying not to lose mine over in Bulgaria, just in case we have to, pick up and go. Add that to challenges with people in our family. Both of us have people on each side that there's been a pretty bad division politically. And around the elections, that got very bad. Then when the vaccines came out, it kind of reared its head again. Then I burned out from work. I was so severely burnt out and exhausted and underpaid and all that piled up at once. It was bad."

Carly and her husband keep moving forward. They have each other and their passions. Being Childfree allows them freedom but still results in pressure from family. Add that to the world being crazy, and the struggle is hard.

"I need to remind myself because I'm not alone. Sometimes I feel like, especially when surrounded by all these people, sometimes my therapeutic thing is to go on the Childfree subReddit and read for a while. And know, you're not alone. You're not alone. It's okay."

7

CATHRYN – A PORTRAIT OF FEAR

Cathryn
37, Female, Single, New Jersey
Bachelor's in Creative Writing
Artist/Unemployed

C athryn is an artist and a musician. She has her own art business doing tissue paper collages to create images for children's rooms and books. This business is just one of three she is getting off the ground. At the same time, she is looking for a "day job" to pay the bills.

Cathryn grew up expecting (and being expected) to have kids but chose the Childfree lifestyle after realizing it was an option:

"I realized that I just didn't have the desire to have my own children. I didn't know that there was a choice. I didn't think about it much when I was growing up. I was a babysitter from the age of 10, and my brother, my little brother, was born when I was like 11 and a half. So, I was always taking care of kids. I was going to a Baptist church that was a little bit conservative. There was no discussion of if you want kids. It would just be, like, that is your role. In lots of sermons, they would talk about becoming a good mother or dad biblically. I always assumed that because I was good with kids, loved kids, and cared about them, I would also be a mother. I was more interested in adoption because I wanted to have lots of kids. I always felt deeply about the kids in the world that don't get a good chance when they're born into circumstances that they have nothing to do with. I've always had that conflicting thought in my mind. I really would weep if I read about kids in poverty.

When I started going to college, my mind was expanding with possibilities. Around that time, I was like 23 or 24, my younger sister got married, and she got pregnant pretty fast. I was very excited for her, but I remember suddenly feeling this huge sense of relief that it wasn't me. When I was younger, I thought I would be the one to get married quickly and start having all the babies. I just remember feeling glad that I didn't meet someone when I was her age. That would have been me. That relief surprised me because I hadn't really thought about it. That is when I realized, wait, I maybe don't actually want to have kids.

I remember it. I looked it up online. This was back in like 2007 or 2008. There wasn't a lot on there. I remember typing in 'women who don't want to have kids' because I thought, am I like the only one? Am I defective or something? I remember reading about other women who made a choice not to have kids. Some people shared that they don't desire to have kids, and that's okay. I was suddenly like, okay, that sounds like me. I don't want to have my own kids. I just care about everybody else's kids. I'll do things to help kids in the world. I will help the children in the world who have very little. Even now today, I still sponsor children who are in poverty. My artwork is geared towards the children's market, but I still, to this day, have that sense of relief that I can choose not to have them."

I asked Cathryn if she would adopt a kid now:

"I thought about it. I was like, well, maybe when I'm 40, and I have my finances together, and I'll want to adopt. But then the longer I've been in this Childfree state of being, I've realized that I don't want to do that either."

Cathryn sees the biggest benefit of being Childfree as a sense of relief and the time it gives her to follow her passions:

"The biggest benefit is the huge sense of relief that I have a choice. I also have my time and mental space free to face my circumstances and build my life the way I want. I've had a lot of struggles over the years, and I just can't imagine having kids on top of that. I can just focus on building my career, building my businesses. One of my favorite things is that I have the time and the mental space to learn whatever I want. I take voice lessons. I'm in choirs, and I have the time to learn a new skill."

Does Cathryn have any regrets about being Childfree?:

"No, so far, and I probably never will. I can't even think of a regret that I could have. I don't think it ever crossed my mind even to regret it because I'm very happy."

I asked Cathryn how her life would be different if she were financially secure. What would she change?:

"I would not change my mind about being Childfree, that's for sure. I would continue building my businesses that have to do with the arts. I wouldn't have to have a day job. That would be like my dream to just be able to choose what I do with my day."

Cathryn is currently juggling starting three businesses with looking for a day job. Right now, she lives with her family and is trying to get her feet on the ground. Her passion is in arts, music, and writing, but she also has to pay the bills. She recently moved to get out of a bad situation and to get some family support. Now she is trying to figure out what her future looks like and how to trust her judgment (which is helped by her decision to be Childfree):

"It's funny because, in light of talking about my Childfree decision at the beginning, I'm now seeing I can trust my own intuition and decision-making. If I'm really unhappy at the thought of doing life a certain way that everyone else expects me to, I'm usually very practical and whimsical, but I don't need the work. I'm not lazy, but I always have this thing in the back of my mind that says I should want to have, like, the typical career. I think that my business ideas are just like pie in the sky or something. But this makes me realize that maybe I need to trust myself more. I'm so happy with my decision not to have kids. It's allowed me so many opportunities over the years—even little things like pouring into my niece and nephew's lives and helping my sister. If I had my own family, that wouldn't be happening. So if I can look at that and say, like, I've trusted myself in that decision. I stuck with it all this time, and I made huge decisions. Maybe if I gave that same amount of trust to my other decisions, like with career business goals or relationship goals, I'll be just as happy."

Cathryn is at a point that is similar to many. She has chosen not to follow the LifeScript™ by being Childfree, but making another choice to be different is hard. Having faith in her choice to run three businesses rather than get a "day job" is hard. The same goes with relationship choices. Trusting your own decisions is hard:

"I don't care what other people think about me being Childfree. I have zero interest in kids. If someone has an opinion about it, it's never going to change my mind. For some reason, with other things like relationships, even starting one to begin with, or the whole financial career path thing, it's like a bomb goes off in my head full of what I should do or what I'm expected to do."

Cathryn did not give anyone else a vote in her decision to be

Childfree. So why does she allow others to weigh in on her other decisions?:

> "That's a good question. I think it's hard with the financial one because I live with my sister and brother-in-law. They took me in after a really bad repetitive use injury from my job. So, there was very little, like, to do for a long time. I couldn't do the job I was doing anymore. So I moved from St. Louis to live with them in Houston and had to do retail for a couple of years. I just couldn't type anymore. I could barely write. All that to say they don't like, give me any pressure. It's not like they were like, you must pay rent now, and you must get on your feet. I just feel like I'm 37, and I've lived with them for like five years now. They have kids who are seven, 12, and 14. I've practically lived with my niece and nephews almost their whole lives. I feel like I should be able to get myself together financially so that I don't have to live with them or rely on them financially. I want my own place. I want in the long-term to be happy in the jobs that I'm doing. I don't know. There's some inward stress about, like, being a burden on them, even though they actively support me and encourage me all the time."

I asked Cathryn if it was a fear of failure or a fear of success that was holding her back:

> "That is actually something I've been wondering lately. I've been reading some books that have been making me question myself. I already know what it feels like to fail miserably multiple times. Not necessarily always because of my fault, but because of just circumstances blowing up in my face, like with the injury. I don't know what it looks like to imagine myself thriving and where my businesses are thriving. Where I'm living my life in the arts, and I can, like, have my own space and also, like, still have my nieces and nephews and sister and brother-in-law over and, like, be able to help them. I don't know what that looks like. It is kind of scary. I want it, but I'm afraid of being disappointed in that. I guess there's the

failure part. I'm afraid of it blowing up in my face too. I don't know if I could handle the disappointment. I'm also, like, really nervous. Like I've never seen myself in that state of being able to be financially, like, on my own feet."

Cathryn's situation is relatively common. We've all had hard times. We've all had things that did not go as planned. Once we get ourselves stable, it can be very challenging to take another chance. The challenge is that, as Childfree individuals, we do have the flexibility to take chances. Fear of the unknown, fear of success, fear of failure all start to build on themselves. Cathryn is currently just looking for any day job as long as it is stable and pays the bills. She has support and is safe now, but taking a leap towards her artistic passions is hard. Rather than following a passion, she has split her time between three ideas and a day job. Why?:

"Part of it is like this fear that you shouldn't put all your eggs in one basket. Part of me is terrified of going back to the poverty level I lived in before. There is also that voice in the back of my head that sometimes comes up... I was amazing in school. I was in gifted level and honors classes my entire life. It feels like as soon as I got out of school, I didn't know how to do life. I just didn't fit in a lot of, like, the expectations or the ways of doing things that seem to come so easy to friends and family members. So, there's this fear that I can't do life or that something is missing or that, for some reason, I just don't have the capabilities of succeeding as everybody else does. So, part of me is afraid of, like, if I don't try all the avenues they're telling me, or that I need to do a career this way. These are people who are telling me to do it this way. I am telling myself that I need to be an entrepreneur, but I'm afraid. What if I'm wrong and that person's right? Or what if that person's right about me and that other person is wrong? So let me try to do all of them, and five might fail, but one might work."

As an entrepreneur myself, I hear Cathryn. There are always

doubts, and it is tough to put yourself and your ideas out there. Some people, such as Cathryn, face that fear by doing a lot of "stuff." The challenge is, to be successful in business, you need to run one idea until it runs out, and then you can try something else. Deliberate focus gets you to your goal, but that does mean putting your eggs in one basket. Having a safety net is good, but you are stuck if the net prevents you from moving forward. It is okay to fail. It is okay to fall. The difference between moving forward and not is just how fast you pick yourself up and try again.

I know Cathryn has the passion, skills, and abilities to do whatever she wants. I hope she can use her success and faith in her decision to be Childfree to push her to accomplish everything else she wants. So, Cathryn, you do you. Live your best life.

8

CINDY – A PORTRAIT OF CARING

Cindy
39, Female, Married, Illinois
Bachelor's in Business
Operations Manager

Cindy is married, works as an operations manager, and loves cats. Cindy and her husband care for her mother and also took care of her father for 18 months before he passed. Caring is at the core of Cindy's heart:

"I'm in Illinois, and it is freezing cold out here right now. I think it was minus-five. I have a little group of stray cats that I take care of. I built little houses for them so that they won't freeze to death."

While she may have considered dating someone who had kids, being Childfree has worked out for her:

"I'm just not a child person and never have been. I never had that calling to have kids. It just really was never in the cards for me... I like my time to be my own. The flexibility to do what I want when I want is very important. It's the same concept with money. I don't want to work my ass off for the rest of my working life for someone else to spend my money. I'd rather choose what I do with my money and having a child isn't important to me... I like caring for other people. So that has nothing to do with not wanting kids. I'm pretty happy in a caregiver role most of the time. I've been like that my whole life."

Being Childfree allows Cindy to live her life best life. When asked what the most significant benefit of being Childfree was, Cindy shared:

"I would say not having to consider how my decisions are going to impact someone else [besides her husband], especially someone else who is smaller may not understand things. My husband and I are very much on the same page on pretty much everything. We're very much alike. We can live a fairly independent life with each other, and I don't have to overthink any single decision that I make."

Cindy enjoys her work as an operations manager but would love more time for travel:

"Work is always at the forefront of my mind when I'm planning my time away. I can't be gone for two weeks at a stretch to go to Greece, to go to Italy. I can be away for a week. Not a problem. Even though I am an ops manager for an engineering company, I keep my hours close to 45 hours per week. So, I have a more balanced daily life than most, but I don't have as much flexibility, you know, for larger chunks of time."

Financial security is more important than travel, and being Childfree helps Cindy and her husband make progress:

"We always want to be financially secure. He and I both grew up with parents that were lower class and worked very blue-collar jobs.

Having financial security has always been very important to both of us. His family filed a number of bankruptcies. We [Cindy's family] never went without, so to speak, we were never living in the best houses. He and I had an agreement very early on that being financially secure was important. We didn't want to have to worry about if we could pay our bills."

Cindy wants to retire at 60, but her husband would like her to retire a bit earlier. Part of this may be due to the age gap (her husband is 52), but they both know Cindy loves working. Cindy has her own challenges, including having lupus, but she tries not to let it hold her back. She has few symptoms besides some back pain. However, it does mean they have to have a good plan and consider long-term care options:

"I already have some mobility issues. I also have lupus. So, I know I have health issues. I do the long-term and short-term disability insurance at work. Even though they are a little expensive, they make sense for me, given I've had back surgeries in the past couple of years and stuff like that. You don't know what's going to happen. So, the plan at this point is to stay independent as long as I can or be independent with the help of my husband. Even though he's older, he's in a little bit better shape... I am a control freak when it comes to my medical care. So, for me, it would be very important to be able to make the decisions myself about where I'm going to go and where I'm going to stay. Who's going to take care of me. I have to be able to trust that person."

Cindy's husband has taken the past two years off from work to care for Cindy's father. Her father was diagnosed with cancer, and, as with many, he needed some support with doctor's visits and healthcare. For 18 months, until her father passed, Cindy's husband was that support. Then, together, Cindy and her husband chose for him to stop working to care for her father:

"My husband's not working right now. That was because of my father. Towards the end of his life, he needed a lot of rides to doctor's appointments for his cancer treatment. It was about an hour, hour and a half each way every week. So, the choice was either I had to quit my job, or he was going to die within weeks. My husband said, well, you make more than I do. I'll step away. I'll be the chauffeur. And he did that with my dad up until the last weeks of his life through COVID and everything."

Even though cutting out an income comes with a cost, Cindy knew it was the right thing to do, and they could afford it:

"It was the right choice ethically for me morally. It wasn't gonna hurt us financially. I mean, could we have saved more, been on a more solid footing? Yeah, sure. But you know, it was someone's life. Literally, I wasn't going to play that game... There is a balance between taking care of someone like my father and retiring early compared to the national average. I made that choice to care for someone else versus to put it towards end financial goals... The money aspect was never really that important."

Being Childfree and in a relatively good financial position allowed Cindy and her husband to choose to take care of her father:

"If I would have had a child, there's no way the money would have cut it. It would have been an absolutely horrific decision to try to make. I probably still would've made the same decision, though. [Being Childfree] allows the ability to do what I want when I want, without having to think about the repercussions too deeply. It is just that this is what I feel like I'm called to be doing, and this is what I'm going to do."

The only debate was who was going to take care of Cindy's father, not if they were going to do it:

"One of us was going to do it. We're going to do it. We discussed if I would miss two days of work, and he would miss two days of work the next week. We went through a number of options. It was going to happen. It was a matter of how it worked out best. In the end, my husband's just like, you know what? We're just going to bounce back and forth. He's like, there's no continuity. With the doctors, you're always gonna be wondering whether you're going or I'll wonder whether I'm going. And he was like, it's just gonna be easier if it's one person and you make more, it makes sense. Even though it makes more sense for me to go with my dad from a medical background standpoint, knowing his history, it made more sense for my husband to walk away from a financial perspective, from his job to do it. I could always be on the phone for phone calls with the doctors. But it's that whole, it was the commuting and sitting and waiting. That's, you know, he made the time investment with that."

I asked Cindy if her father expected them to support him:

"I don't think initially he did. He fought us on it for a bit, but the sicker he got, the more dependent he became. It was not an expectation upfront. He absolutely hated it. We avoided telling him that my husband had quit his job at the start. We just said, oh, his boss is being flexible. One day my husband let it slip that he had [quit his job]. And [my father said] 'that's not what I told you guys to do.' [Cindy replied to her father] We didn't say you told us, we made the decision. Leave it alone."

Being Childfree may have allowed Cindy the financial ability to care, but it is just part of who she is:

"I've lived my life to take care of something. It does not matter if it's a four-legged something or two-legged."

In all my interviews, I ask, "Is there a question I should have asked that I did not?" Cindy responded that after hearing about

caring for her parents, that I should have asked why it was so important. So here's why it was so important for her to care for her parents:

"They took care of me. I was not an easy child. No, I was a nightmare. I was absolutely horrible. They took care of me, and it wasn't
even so much as repayment, but they took care of me. They raised
me to do the right thing. When someone needs you, especially a
family member that close needs you, you do whatever you can to
ensure that people are taken care of when they need you the most.
And I don't think we have enough good stuff like that in the world
where people are doing something just purely for the fact of helping
someone else; it's usually to get something. I think more people
need to do stuff where it's out of kindness, not an expectation, not a
requirement, just out of kindness. That's how I was raised. And I
know they're proud of me. And I know that as much as dad may
have fought the decision, I know he's very proud of the decision we
made. I'm not going to deny it, that's a great feeling, but that's just
the way I was raised."

9

GREG – A PORTRAIT OF LOGIC AND FIRE

Greg
37, Male, Married, Virginia
Bachelor's in Accounting
Corporate Accountant

Greg and his wife are accountants. He is an accountant for a financial firm, and she works for a university. He and his wife have a plan to FIRE (Financial Independence, Retire Early) at 45, and they are well on their way. They have been married for 12 years and enjoy their life with their dog Penny. While it may be a bit of the chicken and the egg as far as determining which came first, it is evident that both Greg's life and work as an accountant are very logical. Even their choice to not have kids has a very logical sound to it:

"I think neither of us were ready to give up our careers to make the commitment that having a kid would require. I know people who work and have kids, but I couldn't see that working out for us. We start work at eight in the morning and end at six or seven at night. It's like, how would that work with the kid? So that was a big factor.

Some financial things come into play as well. Even if we were able to keep our income the same, having kids is an expense. I guess some people can do it without spending too much, but I think in general, it's a fairly hefty financial commitment in addition to the time."

The choice to be Childfree isn't only about time and money for Greg and his wife:

"I think for us, just having the freedom to do what we will and what we're already doing is enough. Maybe our plates are full without kids. I know people talk about how kids bring meaning to their lives. I feel like I would want my life to have meaning first and then have kids. It feels like kicking the can if kids give your life meaning. Like, then it's their problem [kids] to figure out what the meaning of life is. I don't know if there needs to be a meaning to life or if there is, or what it is, but for me, that was something that I'm like, why would I have kids?"

Greg is happy with his life and his progress towards FIRE. He is willing to put in the hours it takes, and not having kids helps the plan. However, he sees the biggest benefits of being Childfree as freedom and the financial impact:

"I think freedom and finances are probably the biggest benefits. In theory, we travel whenever we want. In reality, we can travel whenever we can get away from work. So we don't have that extra restriction of the school schedule, who will watch the kids, or whatever. And then the financial impact. We're 37 and hoping to be done working at 45. I think that would get pushed out a couple of years if we were taking care of a kid, funding college, or whatever."

Greg does not have any regrets about being Childfree and sees it as a different path:

"I wouldn't say regrets. I think, you know, there are times when our friends come over, and they have kids, and their kids are cute and whatever, but I think that's fine for them, and this can be fine for us. But, you know, it would be a different path. I don't think it would necessarily be a better path for us. So I'm going to say no to regrets."

Greg and his wife are on their path to Financial Independence (FI). The bonus of FI is that you get to do what you want to do. It does not necessarily mean the traditional retirement, but it is a different way of life. Here is what Greg envisions their FI life to look like:

"I would not work at my current job. I'm not sure exactly how not working would impact me. I know that for many people, you work hard for many years, and then you stop working, and it's not what they expected. So, I could certainly see myself doing something like a part-time job. I think we would both enjoy volunteering more... Volunteering more, maybe with something like Habitat for Humanity or a local soup kitchen. Maybe being a bigger part of our neighborhood community. Travel would be a big part of our lives."

Greg has built in giving to charities as both a goal and part of his FIRE plan:

"As part of our current financial goals, we are saving enough to be able to give more than we are now. Giving generously is certainly something I'd like to do. I'm currently planning that when I get to our FIRE number, I will work one more year and bank all of that for charity... I want to be able to have an impact that's noticeable on my community."

Greg has always had FIRE as a goal:

"I've always been interested in retiring early since I started working. When I started, I think I had 55 as a goal, and that was like from day one. I found the Dave Ramsey group first and then ChooseFI. I didn't spend very long in the Dave Ramsey group. I'm not sure how I found it on Facebook and never felt like, oh, this is the path I'm following, but it did bring me to ChooseFI, which has been more beneficial."

Greg credits his parents with setting the best foundation for him. They came to the U.S. as immigrants, and he shared:

"My parents did all the work and made the sacrifices. As a result, I'm getting the benefits. Growing up with that sacrifice and their thriftiness is part of my background and my focus on saving."

In the end, is Greg happy with his life?:

"Yes. Overall, I am happy with my life. I am looking forward to being able to be generous with our time and money in the future."

10

GUSTAVO – A PORTRAIT OF WORRY

Gustavo
27, Single, Male, Texas
Master's in Architecture
Drafter and Clerical Support

Gustavo is 27, single, and living with his parents. He has a Master's degree in architecture, but for now, he is just gaining experience doing drafting and clerical support and working his way up. He wants to live on his own but is worried about his job not paying enough and the impact on his family. He wants more from his life, but is concerned about the steps it will take to get there. He would love to run his own company, but that can be scary. He followed many of the "normal" steps, but isn't where he wants to be:

"I went through the typical path. Everyone tells you to go to college. I went for six years to get my Master's of architecture. I was used to succeeding all the time. I was the type of person where I'm used to succeeding academically. But the problem with me looking back is that I was always a full-time student my whole life. I never got exposure to the real world after graduating from college. That's when I started to struggle for the first time. I had to accept the fact that I could not achieve anything. I cannot get everything that I want.

When I graduated, I had six months before I had to pay student loans. I needed to get a job somewhere. I applied to a few architecture firms, but I didn't get anything back. I got one interview with a recruiter. But it did not go anywhere because I did not have experience. Things are not just handed to you. Like nothing. I've already learned that. So after four months of searching, I started to look for something else that's not related to architecture. I had to find something to begin paying off student loans."

Gustavo worked in tech support for a while, which helped him learn personal skills and pay off his student loans. It wasn't what he wanted or his original plan, but it worked.

So why did Gustavo decide to be Childfree?:

"Looking back at my past, I've always been one of those kids who put focus on school. My main focus was on college. People asked me if I wanted to have kids or not. I was more focused on my school, so I never questioned it. Later, I came across two videos that helped. It started with one particular video from Australia's Insight [a current affairs television program]. The topic was being childfree. The host interviewed all these different people about their experiences of if they don't want kids, or they want kids and all these different stories. I was just blown away by hearing all these people's different insights. That was my first exposure to hearing that it is an option you can choose. Then later, I came across other channels. In particular, I've seen Hannah from Wife Without Kids.

So I guess to sum it up, the reason I don't want kids is I guess the financial one is a big one for me. The second one is the freedom that I have. I don't have to worry about having kids. I can just relax. I can take a breath after working, and I can focus on finding ways to be able to move on and to make progress towards being more financially stable. I hear all these different stories from people who struggle financially. I don't know how they do it, and I don't want to go through something like that at all. And also, another reason is just; I've never desired fatherhood. I never desired to be a parent. I don't desire that typical life that people tell you to do."

Gustavo's experiences are typical. He followed the standard Life-Script™ and went to college and planned on getting that great job out of college. That did not happen as expected. He made the best of it and worked hard to get out of student loans. Like many others, he did not initially realize that it was a choice when it came to having kids. Having kids is just another part of the LifeScript™ that is expected. Luckily, he took the time to reflect and learn what made sense for him.

What does Gustavo see as the biggest benefit of being Childfree?:

"I've got time for myself. I guess the freedom part of it. I can focus on more important things in my life. I'm learning when I'm not working my full-time job. I'm working on proving my skills until I find a better job."

Does he have any regrets about his choice to be Childfree?:

"I don't think twice about it. I like the life that I have, even though it's not the best, I know I have it better than most people. People are struggling with kids. Even people who don't have kids are struggling. Sometimes I forget to be grateful for what I have. So many people I know wish they were in a position where I'm at."

So what does Gustavo want from his life at this point?:

"I guess I want to be my own boss to be able to just build digital content for clients. I want to make enough for myself and to not rely on anybody anymore, especially from the struggle of finding a job. So I want to work where I am my own boss. I want to be able to just work on my laptop. As long as I have internet and my computer, I want to be able to do my work. I just want to take my computer anywhere I want to go. In other words, I want to be able to travel and just not be tied down and stuck in one place."

Gustavo is debt-free and has an emergency fund. What is holding him back from following his dreams? What does he need to do now?:

"I guess, more than anything, I just need to enjoy life a little bit more and not take my life so seriously. I always feel like I'm just stuck or financially not in the best situation. That's why work crosses my mind so many times. When I'm not working on the working, I'm focusing on working on my way to find a better position where I make enough money for me to live. But at the same time, I need to enjoy life as well. Sometimes I just go to restaurants by myself, which I enjoy. Even going to some parties and just walking around and being somewhere where there's nature helps a lot. But even then, the social part is tricky because everybody doesn't have time as they used to. It's not like college or high school, where you always have to see everybody. Now everything is different. I feel like everybody's growing up way too fast."

Overall, Gustavo wants to start enjoying his life. So was there a time when he truly enjoyed his life or is this just the start of it?:

"There were moments that I enjoyed. For example, I got the opportunity to study abroad in Italy. That completely changed my view on so many things. I never felt so happy in my life. Experiencing a different culture, different norms, seeing all these different cities and places, and seeing a whole different world. I even got to travel and visit other countries such as Spain, Germany, the Vatican, and San Marino. I saw all these different places and got to embrace a whole different culture, different world, a whole different lifestyle.

They're not materialistic. They're not luxurious, but I was very happy with the life I was living. I was very happy. I had no stress. I felt free and liberated. And I felt the sense of community because it's very communal. It's not like you're in the States where everything is all divided."

If Gustavo was so happy living in a different world, outside the U.S., why doesn't he move?:

"Well, there are so many different factors. One of them is my parents are an issue. I mean, they're not an issue, and I love them dearly. The real issue between them is that they are kind of breaking apart. There's gonna be a time when they're not going to live together. It's going to affect everything. On the financial part, I have to take care of my mother, of course. She's the one who will be, if it does happen, who's going to be living with me. If it does happen, I will lose the financial stability that I have right now. If my parents end up separating, things are going to be different. It doesn't affect how they love me.

It's just going to change everything. I guess, financially, it will affect a lot of things. And I feel like all the parts are going to be on me. I want to move, to be able to help myself and then help my parents out as well because they're good right now but they're just like back and forth. I'm not involved in their drama, but it is gonna affect me as well as an adult child."

Is Gustavo's mom expecting him to take care of her, or is he doing this because it is what he thinks she needs?:

"The second part, I think it is what she needs. She's at retirement age. If she is going to be on her own, she needs support. I mean, it's, it's complicated for me. The whole thing, the whole drama with my parents, is just what's preventing me from growing because I don't know what's going to happen. And sometimes divorces can be messy. I've been told you cannot prepare for what might happen. And that concerns me because when it does happen, everything will be different. My financials are going to be different as well. I feel like that's what is preventing me from growing. Yeah. It's, it's complicated. I don't know. I don't know if I'm overthinking it too much or not."

Gustavo probably is overthinking things. As the classic saying goes, "Worrying is like paying a debt you don't owe." He is already paying for what might (or might not) happen in the future. Like many Childfree individuals, he has taken on supporting his mother. It is why he hasn't moved out and why he isn't taking a chance to start his own company. He fears what will happen financially, even though it might not ever happen. I asked him why all of this falls onto his shoulders:

> "Well, I mean, how I picture it is as if it was just my mother and me, and she's retired. She has her Social Security, but that's hers. As for me, I have to make enough income to just live on my own. Ideally, I just want to live by myself and not deal with anybody."

Worrying about things that might happen might just be part of Gustavo's nature:

> "I am the person who overthinks things. It's just like, I think about all the scenarios before they happen. I think it's just the fears. I just do not want to be in a situation where I'm just stuck. I'm having to worry so much about how just to survive and live."

11

HEATHER – A PORTRAIT OF PERSISTENCE

Heather
34, Female, Single, Colorado
Grad Student in Conservation Biology

Heather is working hard on her Master's degree in Conservation Biology and her focus is on protecting birds. She has no debt and is paying her way through her degree (with the hope of no student loans). Heather has done some amazing things, starting with serving in the Peace Corps, and has been able to both enjoy life and give back. Her portrait isn't one of money but of persistence. Heather explains:

"I don't think enough people understand that financially, it's also hard out there for people who don't have kids. This isn't the suffering Olympics... Lots of Childfree people did the math and realized that a kid would take them from just floating to drowning."

Heather didn't decide to be Childfree:

"I don't know that it was a decision. I've never really wanted kids."

It wasn't until later in her life that she even learned the term Childfree:

"The first time I heard the phrase Childfree I was like, oh, there is a word for it. It was never a conscious decision. I just found out that there was suddenly a term for it that I had never been using."

Time is the most significant benefit of being Childfree for Heather:

"Your time is your own. You're not tied down by any one thing, which has enormous benefits. Especially if you're still single... You have so much more free time. More opportunities come along that you can take advantage of. Maybe there is a job or something in a different state across the country or whatever, and you want to do it. But if you had kids or something like that, you definitely wouldn't. That's important with what I do in biology. There are a lot of good opportunities that pop up that are on the other side of the country. It may be short-term, like a six-month gig, but it's a good networking opportunity and chance to connect with really good people. If I'd had kids, I would not [take the opportunity]. I don't think I would still have a career [in biology] if I had kids. Honestly, all the women that I went to school with, if they had kids, they're not doing this anymore."

Heather has worked hard to get to where she is now. She currently works during summer or school breaks while finishing her Master's degree. She isn't living a life of luxury, but being debt-free and cutting corners does mean that she can make progress:

"I live with friends, and that's how I'm able to continue to afford to go to school. I am incredibly fortunate not to have any debt. I think I'm probably one of the few people I know that has zero debt. Everything's all paid off. I, fortunately, did not have to take out any loans when I got my undergrad. For the last few years, I was just squir-reling away money like crazy to pay for grad school. I haven't had to take out any loans so far... I'm living off savings because I'm a student right now until summer when I can go get another job and kind of hoard money and squirrel it away and then live off of that again in the winter. So, it's feast or famine, but because I don't have any debt, I can make it work. If I had debt that was eating into that more, it would be a very different story. So, I don't think the whole feast and famine thing works. It's not sustainable long-term, and I definitely know that, but it works for now. I have a place to stay. I'm going through school, and fortunately, I'm not paying an extra thou-sand dollars a month or whatever for loans."

I asked Heather whether she intentionally stayed out of debt or if it was just something that happened. She responded that it was a combination of luck and being careful about what she spent her money on:

"I did get lucky when I did my undergrad. It was like right before I think the student debt crisis really hit. And I was fortunate enough that my grandparents had put aside some money for a college savings account. So I did have that as well to dip into. I was incred-ibly lucky that I just squeaked through and didn't have to take out any loans. My siblings did have to [take out loans], but they also went to a more expensive school. So that is also a little part of it. And I've always been incredibly careful about what I spend money on. My car is an old junker, but it's all paid off. I don't have any crazy expensive hobbies. I don't have any crippling addiction to high-end fashion. I don't even know what I would spend money on if it wasn't just, like, food and bills and my dog." [Heather's dog is a tiny village dog she brought back from her time in the Peace Corps.]

I asked Heather if she thought she should do anything differently with her life:

"I mean, there's probably all kinds of things that I should do differently, but I don't know that it is all feasible. I mean, I probably should have a 401(k). I probably should have, like, a plan for five to 10 years... I'm a student. When you're only employed for a few months out of the year, before you go back to school, you're just like, what bill do I have to pay today? What grocery bill do I have to pay today? You can't afford to think about five to 10 years. I think five to 10-year planning is more career-oriented. What would you ideally like to be doing in five to 10 years? Because five to 10 years financially doesn't make any sense when you're just trying to make ends meet. When any dollar that comes in is already earmarked for, you know, paying tuition or paying your bills or paying groceries."

Heather is right on. Heather is 34 and is focusing on school just like she should be. She is working hard to make ends meet and stay out of debt. It can be common to get stuck in comparing our finances to someone else's or expected "norms." People read articles that say by X age you should have done Y. Maybe it is that you should have a certain amount in a 401(k) or, some other measure. All those measures don't matter. The only person we should measure against is ourselves. Heather understands that and deserves credit for having her priorities straight.

Heather has cut back on work to focus on school but plans to return to work in the summer. Finding temporary work to pay for school can be challenging:

"One of the problems with doing a lot of temporary work like that is hiring usually doesn't start until January and February when more jobs get posted. So, I'm hoping stuff will start popping up in the next couple of months that I can apply for. But it is very kind of last-minute sort of stuff. I've had jobs come through in the past. So, within like a week, I'll get a notice, talk to someone and then they're like, yeah, come on up. And it happens very quickly. So, planning five to 10 years for anything is very odd when I don't know if I will have a job in June or not."

Heather's goal is to find a permanent job in her field, which is challenging:

"When you're living six months to six months, goals feel very nebulous right now. I just want to finish my degree and find a job somewhere. I don't have anything really beyond that. I don't know that I can really say, my goal in 10 years is to have a down payment on a house. That feels astronomical, like wherever the James Webb telescope is, it's past that. That's how far out that feels. I'd like to have a job, and that's kind of it."

Heather is following her passions. Once she gets that job in conservation, she plans on doing it as long as possible. Retirement isn't a goal or thought now. Then again, part of the reason Heather has trouble getting a permanent job is that those in the positions aren't retiring.

Childfree Wealth to Heather reflects benefits that are a combination of time and money:

"I think time is probably more important [than money], but I don't want to say money isn't as important. You can make less go further when you don't have kids. I have taken jobs that are pretty crappy-paying because I don't have student loans. Maybe if I was childfree but did have loans, I might not have been able to do that. I think I'm in a unique boat, and I acknowledge that. I have been able to take jobs that pay kind of crappy because it would be good work experience or with people that I want to work for."

Heather doesn't want anything fancy, just to live her own, authentic life:

"I just wanted enough to kind of take care of my needs. It would be nice if I could have some kind of a savings account or retirement plan, but that's hard when all you're doing is making ends meet. That's kind of what it comes down to right now... If you can get your-

self sheltered, fed, and clothed, and have a running car, you're probably doing pretty damn good. That's kind of what I would just like
life to continue being. Ideally, I'd be able to live on my own, but I
can't afford that. So, I live with friends, but otherwise, it's pretty
good."

Heather is following her own path. Living with friends may not
be ideal, but it is realistic. Her parents grew up in a different financial
world, yet they still encourage Heather to get a "good job" and a
house:

"It absolutely doesn't work like that anymore. I'm living with friends
in my thirties. And we're all still just hanging on, doing our own
thing. They [her parents and others] think living with friends at this
age is extremely strange. I've seen articles in the last few months
talking about buying homes with friends. You've got groups of
friends living together because that's all anyone can afford. They
[her parents] are shocked and horrified that this is what things are
like. And it's like, no one can afford anything else. This is what we
can afford. So that's how we live. That's what we do. And the advice
that is being given by them is completely irrelevant. It does not
apply to anyone's situation anymore because a house, where we [her
family] bought a house 15 years ago, would have been, you know,
mid-300 [$350K] and, or upper 300 [$399K+] probably. And now it's
closer to a million. That's insane. No one can afford that kind of
down payment. Ridiculous."

Even given the hard work she has put in (or maybe because of it),
Heather doesn't have regrets about her Childfree life:

"If I had kids, I would not be able to still be working in my field like
this. I would have had to have given up a long time ago and just
taken anything to have a regular paycheck. So I'm fine grinding it
out. I'm 34, so I've done close to 10 years of seasonal fieldwork. I'm

trying to network and talk to people and gain experience while going back to grad school. So I'm fine with that because it's interesting. And I still enjoy it."

12

JACY – A PORTRAIT OF COMPROMISE

Jacy

28, Female, Single, Texas

Some College in Civil Engineering

Contract Administrator

J acy is 28, single, and she grew up in a small town in the panhandle of Texas "where we have more cows than people." She is fortunate to work for the state government, which offers excellent job security and a pension (which is very rare now). Fortunately, her job allows her to work from anywhere, and Jacy recently moved to support her aging grandparents. Of course, it isn't ideal, but Jacy was willing to move and compromise to meet her family obligations.

Jacy has a wide variety of reasons for choosing to be Childfree. These include family, finances, and medical issues:

"With the background of my parents, I had kind of a rough upbringing. My parents did split up eventually, which was a good thing for everybody involved, but my mom suffers from mental illness pretty badly. So, I know that can run in the family. I have paid a lot of money for therapy for that reason. So, the biggest reason for me to be Childfree is to stop generational curses, for lack of a better word. I don't want to screw kids up. Kids are a lifetime responsibility, and frankly, I don't want that kind of responsibility. I don't even own pets because I prefer to have the freedom to do what I want when I want and not have to worry about anybody but myself.

I always tell my parents, like I didn't ask to be here. Y'all brought me here, and I wouldn't want a child to feel that way. I also see the financial hardships of having a child. I had stepkids at one point in my life, and that drove home the expense side of things. They're expensive. Daycare is expensive. School is expensive, and I work for the state. I'm not super wealthy or anything, and I don't want to struggle. I know I can financially support myself. I'm comfortable with the money I'm making now and where I'm at. I would like to continue that. I love to travel, and kids make that hard. And lastly, I do have health issues that could be passed on to a child, as I have autoimmune issues and things like that. With my autoimmune stuff, they don't know where it comes from. They think it might be genetic, but they're not for sure. So far, I'm the only one in my family who has it, but it is possible to pass that along to a child. I couldn't bear to do it because I know what I live with every day. And I wouldn't want to put that on another person."

Jacy mentioned that she had stepkids for a while. For this book, I have defined Childfree as "not having kids, and not planning on having kids." I asked Jacy if kids were an option in the future:

"I'm open to the possibility of it. Well, I guess it would kind of have to start out with deceit [as her current relationship did], and I didn't know about them. If I fell in love with the person and found out they had kids, I might think about it. I am dating someone now, and he does have a child, but that has posed problems already. I don't know if that's going to end up as a long-term relationship or not. And if it doesn't, I don't think I would be open to dating someone with kids again."

As someone who is Childfree and has been married for 12 years, I can't get my head around Childfree dating. It is a challenge that I'm very happy I don't have to face. Jacy's dating situation intrigued me, to say the least. She has grown stronger in her stance to be Childfree over the years, yet she was dating someone with a kid. I asked her if the fact that he has a child is a dealbreaker for her:

> "The way their custody and everything is set up, he doesn't have his son all the time. So, when I see him, his son is not always there. I suppose if it were to move in together and get married and things like that, it might be different. So that's definitely a conversation we've got to have."

I've come to accept the concept of "compatible baggage" in a relationship. The bottom line is that we all have baggage that we bring into a relationship. The key to a healthy relationship is accepting someone else's baggage and not trying to change them. We each have different things that we are willing to compromise on and accept. Is Jacy willing to compromise, and is having a kid "compatible baggage"?:

> "At this point, no. I know that sounds hypocritical because the man I am seeing does have a child, but I became set in my decision after we started dating. We were kind of already deep in the trenches of a relationship. So, it's difficult for me because I have strong feelings for him, and I love him. Don't get me wrong; I love kids. It's not that I'm a child-hater, and I love his son as well. It's just very hard to envision a lifetime with the child. So, I guess this is kind of jump-starting questions I need to ask and conversations I need to have with myself and him."

Jacy continued:

> "I struggle with conflict. I'm not a big fan of it. I struggle with even facing it. So I guess I will kind of hem and haw around things until I

get to the point where I can't. And yeah, that is an issue looking forward here. But if I step back and say, I'm single and I'm looking for a partner, then, no, children are not compatible baggage."

I feel for Jacy. She's solidified her Childfree choice over the past year and a half. Part of the reason her choice solidified was dating someone with Children in combination with her medical issues:

"That [dating someone with kids] in part, and then also health issues this year have been really hard for me. So, I'm trying to get a grasp on a lifestyle that, like, a diet and exercise lifestyle that benefits my autoimmune issues. And then thinking about if I were to get pregnant with a child, that would increase the side effects of my autoimmune issues, which would put me in so much more pain for nine months, and then that spiraled into thinking about actual childbirth. I don't want to go through that. It just sounds horrible and miserable. So, I guess all of that kind of stacked up together to solidify my decision to be Childfree."

Jacy sees being single and Childfree as "a nightmare truly." But, even with that "nightmare," the benefits of being Childfree outweigh the challenges. She sees the biggest benefit as freedom:

"For me, it's freedom. I mean, if I want to wake up at noon, I can wake up at noon. If I want to stay out until three o'clock in the morning, I can, and if I want not to cook a meal, if I want to eat chips or, you know, junk food, I don't have to worry about feeding a child or ensuring that they're getting to school or daycare or whatever obligations. So it is the freedom to be able to do what I want to when I want to, and not have to have someone depending on me, or have someone to worry about."

I asked Jacy about her goals and dreams. Her job now pays well, is stable, and has a pension. That is hard to pass up in this job market. But, if she had her choice, she would go in a different direction:

"It would be completely different from the career path I chose. I love the beauty industry. I would love to own a salon, and that's not a super lucrative business. I understand that. But if I were thinking about doing what I want to do, what I love to do, that's what I would do. If I were going to do something that would grant me the life I would like to live, I would probably work in engineering. I am going to school for engineering to obtain a civil engineering degree. In that career path, I would open an engineering firm to do the work with partners that I deal with every day. I see what these people are being paid every day. And I know that that career path would allow me to live the life that I would like to live."

Jacy explained that she had to sacrifice her dreams and put herself second to help her family:

"I'm the oldest of my family, and two years ago, I moved back up here in the panhandle and have sacrificed a lot of my time for my grandparents. And that's another reason to be childfree is not to have to put that obligation on someone. Not that I feel like we are obligated to take care of our parents because, as I said, I didn't choose to be here. They chose to have me, but that has put into perspective that it's a big burden to put on somebody else. And I don't live with them or anything like that. They live one block over from me. So, it's kind of like for every little thing, my phone is ringing. I'm grateful to have the opportunity to be here for them. I know they won't be here forever, but at the same time, I've also lost a few years of my life. I've given my younger years to caring for them in a manner which they can't care for themselves. And it also, like, takes a physical toll on my body because they still live in a house. So many things that my granddad used to be able to do, he can't. So, all of the yard work and the house maintenance and things of that nature have fallen to me because the rest of my family wouldn't step in. They wouldn't help."

What Jacy is experiencing is somewhat the norm. It is normal enough that I classify it as part of the Childfree Financial BINGO. It goes like this: "You don't have kids so you can take care of..." It is sometimes money, sometimes time. I asked Jacy if it was expected of her:

"Was I expected to do it? No, I offered. I was driving up here on the weekends to help them with big projects. I came up and stayed the weekend and noticed that they were struggling more than they let on. So, at that point, I started coming up almost every weekend. And so, it just made sense for me to move back here. I think I was looking for a change from where I was living at the time, and I had the freedom to work anywhere in the state. So, I offered to move back to be there for them... I love them so much. Don't get me wrong. And I'm grateful that I can be here for them, but at the same time, I miss my total and complete freedom. I could tell them no. Or I could say I'm busy, but who else do they have?"

It is not costing Jacy a lot of money, but her time and freedom are tied up in helping her grandparents. It is just another compromise she has had to make. I asked her what she would change if she could:

"I would like to have an impact eventually. I don't exactly know what that is right now, but I feel like I'm called to do more than just what I'm doing right now. So, I definitely could change that. I could reach out to organizations, volunteer my time, volunteer my skills, you know, and help people in need. Because I feel like we have so many in this world who need so much, and I may not be able to help financially, but I know that I could help in other ways."

I would argue that Jacy is already impacting her grandparents and her family. It may not feel the same as another impact, but it is essential. Jacy has had to make some compromises to help them, but it is worth it.

Being Childfree allows us to choose what we want to do with our life. We may not be living our ideal life now, but we have the freedom and flexibility to change. We have to choose what we are willing to compromise and why. Jacy is doing a stable job and providing for her future, which compromises her dreams. Jacy moved and is taking care of her grandparents, but the compromise (in location mostly) is worth it.

What about compromising and accepting compatible baggage in a relationship? After the interview, Jacy reached out to me to share that she did some soul-searching and decided it is not worth compromising her choice to be Childfree for a relationship. She's back on the dating market, but now at least, she knows what she is looking for, even if it is challenging.

13

JESSE – A PORTRAIT OF INTENTIONAL BALANCE

Jesse
35, Male, Married, Colorado
Bachelor's in Education
Indie Video Game Designer

Jesse and his wife live in an RV in Colorado. He is a self-employed video game developer, and she works in healthcare. They have been married for ten years, are Childfree, and have two cats. Jesse and his wife have made being Childfree part of their plan of intentional balance:

"We are past the Analysis Paralysis stage, which kept us from seriously pursuing anything interesting or extraordinary for a few years after we were married and financially stable. Once we decided to make our Childfree life plans concrete, I quit my job to pursue a career in arts/entertainment. My wife has her eyes set on quitting healthcare soon to travel the continent together in our RV and work on the road. These are things we would never have considered if we had children."

Jesse started his life by spending almost a decade in education and as an elementary school teacher. He enjoyed the job and the kids, and they weren't set on a Childfree life from the start. It wasn't until a couple of years ago (when they were about 33 and already married for eight years) that they decided to be Childfree:

> "Originally, we didn't make any proclamations or decisions [about being Childfree]. When my wife and I first started dating, we both kind of had it in our minds that we wanted between two and three kids. It was something that we hadn't given much thought to. We just had never been in serious relationships that got to the point where you started thinking about children. Then, I started working as an elementary school teacher, and my wife was working in a residential setting with teenagers as a social worker. So, we got a lot of it [kids] out of our system. We saw parents' struggles and their wins and things like that. We started thinking, is this something we want to sign ourselves up for? As we started to think about it more seriously, we both came to the realization, like, well, that's not really for us."

Freedom is what Jesse sees as the biggest benefit of being Childfree. They were able to move to Colorado, Jesse started his own gaming company, and his wife was able to start a new career. In addition to being Childfree, he credits Mr. Money Mustache with putting them on the path to financial independence:

> "I've been reading Mr. Money Mustache since 2012 or 2013, pretty much right after he kicked his site off. One of the articles that he wrote that stuck with me was to build the life that you want to retire to. Regardless of whether you're financially independent or not, start living that way and see how much you like it. Over the last ten or so years, that's exactly what we've done. I am to a point where I would not change much of anything at all. They refer to it often as the boring middle when you're saving for retirement, and you're not close enough to your goals to cause any excitement. You're past the

honeymoon period of wow; look at how much I'm saving. That's kind of where I am. I can work very consistently and meet the goals that I want vocationally or avocationally."

Jesse isn't sitting around and doing nothing. He has a set of goals and is intentional in everything he does:

"I'm very intentional. I work on my game every day. I walk every day. I lift [weights] twice a week only because my body doesn't respond well to lifting every day. I need more recovery than that. I don't have weekly goals per se because my days all kind of blend together. There's not a weekday in this style of living that I've chosen. I like it that way. I do have monthly goals that I set for myself. I put in 83 hours on my game because it works out to a thousand a year. And I feel like that's a good goal for my mental health. I want to walk 83 miles a month as well. I set a goal for this year that I wanted to between my hours worked and my miles walked, I wanted to reach 2022, which is what that works out to. So as far as financially, the goals kind of take care of themselves when you live as consistently as we do. We do kind of technically have some savings goals. For this month we are trying to cut down on our food spending a little bit. We do a little bit more bulk cooking and things like that. Socially, we have goals. We try to talk to our family a certain amount, and I stay in contact with my best friend who lives in Texas. I try to read as much as I can in my off time when I'm feeling it."

To top all of that off, Jesse has now completed NaNoWriMo twice. For those unfamiliar, it is a nonprofit program designed to support writers. The name stands for National Novel Writing Month, which is November every year. The goal is to write 50,000 words towards a novel, and he has done it twice.

Jesse is living what I call a FILE (Financial Independence, Live Early) life. Many are familiar with FIRE (Financial Independence, Retire Early), where the goal is retirement. Retirement is an on/off switch for work. FILE is more of a dimmer switch for work. Jesse and his wife have made decisions in their life to allow them both to live the life they want and follow their passions. Jesse wants to make a "mark" on the world with his game and work, working hard to do that. They have chosen to live in an RV (which I could never do with our two English Mastiffs) and found a balance between making and spending money. They have a retirement plan in process, but the goal isn't the traditional retirement, but just a quality of life. Jesse's intentional balance is like having that FILE dimmer switch set just right.

I heard much of my own story in Jesse's. I shared that my wife and I have embraced a "Gardener and the Rose" approach to life. The principle is simple. There are times when we each need to be either the gardener or the rose in couples. The gardener's job is to provide all the support for the rose to grow and shine. It is not about gender or gender roles. As of this writing, I'm the gardener, so my wife can grow in her profession (we just moved 1,200 miles to make that happen). We take turns as the gardener and the rose, and Jesse said that it fits them also:

> "That [the gardener and the rose] sounds like a carbon copy of our story. We started dating when I was 20, and she was 18, so I graduated before she did. I worked as a teacher for a couple of years while she finished her education and then went into her Master's program. For the first three, four years, I was the breadwinner. Then she started working, and I made the jump to instructional design, so she was the breadwinner for a bit. Then I was making good money in instructional design, so she jumped to a less stressful, lower-paying job. When we moved to Colorado, I took some time off to get my head right. She started working at the hospital and started making good money. That's where we are now. Maybe it'll be my turn next to make more money for us, but we've always kind of maintained between 30 and 60% savings rate. So, it's given us a lot of options and the ability to do what we want."

Being Childfree and supportive allows a couple to achieve some fantastic things. However, it wasn't always easy for Jesse and his wife on their journey to financial independence:

"When I first discovered the FIRE movement and first started caring about that sort of thing, I had $70,000 in student loans. I was making $35,000 a year, and for my first year teaching, my wife wasn't working. We were living in a tiny little apartment. There were many things about my life that were like screaming emergencies. So it gave me a lot of incentive to save and cut back. We needed to be minimalists. We needed to do these things because we can't live like this forever."

Now that they have achieved financial independence, their life has changed:

"My mind has completely shifted. I could live like this for a long, long time and expect to. So, I don't get caught up on the minute details of oh my gosh; we spent an extra hundred dollars on beer this year compared to last year. There's so much fat in our lifestyle. It may sound funny to most people, coming from someone who lives in an RV and our annual budget is like $26,000 or whatever, but there's fat to trim. We do live a cushy lifestyle, and it's kind of embarrassing even to admit that. We've been very intentional about things for so long that it's kind of like habit now. We're not worried about anything in our control. You know, there's always the things that could go wrong, health-wise or familial issues or whatever, but we've kind of reached the autopilot stage."

They are happy living in their RV and not worrying about money much. They don't have debt, and it is okay to live on one salary. Jesse's game may make good money someday, but there are no guarantees. He has learned to give himself grace and not beat himself up if he does not make his goals. He makes progress every day, and as long as he is on track for his goals, he's happy:

"I'm pretty close to the track that I want to be on. I feel like any more anxiety or effort put toward reaching goals could be counterproductive or make me feel like I'm not doing a good enough job. One of the things I had to learn right away when becoming self-employed was learning how to give myself a little grace and cut myself a little slack. I've always been kind of one of those obnoxious high-achieving types. And so, if I'm not the best at something right away, I can beat myself up for it pretty hard. I try not to do that now that I need to be more, a little more well-balanced."

I give Jesse credit. He is a lot further than I am at this point. I enjoy what I do, but when I'm staring at my goal of writing 2,000 words today, and nothing is coming, it can be devastating.

Jesse focuses on leaving an "impact" on people's lives. It does not truly matter where or how, but he wants to leave that impact by the time he goes (and I'm sure he will):

"I think that our time here is very important. Our life shouldn't be something done unintentionally. So to me, my legacy should be more to help people to live intentionally. I want to leave my impact and thumbprint on people's lives after reading or playing a game I've created. Or maybe remembering some conversation that we've had or some blog posts that I made. Something that makes people kind of rethink living their life on automatic, or just going through the motions, or wasting their time with things that in the end they're not going to think are very important."

14

JOSIE – A PORTRAIT OF BEING LOST

Josie
25, Female, Single, California
Currently working on a Bachelor's degree
Customer Service

Josie started her discussion with me, describing how she ran away from home at 17 to escape an abusive household. She was trying to get from Louisiana to California. She got as far as Texas, and it wasn't until months later that she was legally allowed to leave and would end up reaching California. Since then, she has been a bit lost (by her own admission) and struggling to get unstuck.

Josie chose to be Childfree at about 15:

"I would say it probably happened around when I was 15. That's when I was officially diagnosed as neurodivergent. And before that, I'd always just been like the weird kid... When I was a little kid, I told my mom I would have a bunch of kids when I grew up. And then when the diagnosis came, it was like, well, if I do have any kids they are going to have a lot of genetic problems. Not just mentally, but most likely physically as well. And I'm just not in a good place, you know, physically, mentally to take care of them."

The biggest benefit of being Childfree for Josie is that no one is relying on you:

"Not having anybody else to take care of besides yourself. If you have a partner, you obviously help take care of them, and they'll help take care of you. But with a kid, it's just that you have to provide everything for them. They completely rely on you for everything. If you don't have the finances to take care of them, they're not going to understand as they're just a baby. They don't know how the world works."

Josie does not regret being Childfree and is currently working on getting sterilized. Josie now lives with her friend's family and is happy raising her chickens (and two VERY vocal roosters). Josie considers herself a storyteller and loves to write and animate. However, story-telling is on hold as she works her way through school doing clerical work and customer service. She has been at the job for seven years but is still just making over minimum wage:

"I'm getting a steady income. It's slightly above minimum wage. So, I guess I'm doing pretty good there. I'm trying to learn a new language and trying to further my education. I'm doing the best I can right now."

Josie received an inheritance when her father passed and invested it in a construction business just before COVID-19 hit:

"I invested my inheritance into a business in the construction field. That never really took off because COVID came immediately after. The business is still around. They're doing work, but it's just not nearly as much as it would be if COVID had never happened. So I've went from relying on that to take off, to trying to get a degree that I can use to further myself."

The business isn't currently bringing in income for Josie. But, even though it was a significant investment, Josie does not regret it:

"I don't regret the investment. If I had known COVID was coming, I probably would have purchased a house where it's not such a high population density."

Now Josie is looking at a career in banking or accounting. Even though she is a creative person at heart, she is "good with numbers and math" to the point where that might be her future. She has been at her job long enough that they rely on her regularly for interpretations of documents sent from customers and billing decisions. It isn't glamorous, and her current position takes it all out of her. It is good that being Childfree allows her the benefit of having more time for herself:

"After working for eight hours, getting screamed at by customers, and trying to read documents all day, sometimes, I choose to be lazy when I get home from work. I don't have to take care of anything or anyone. I, of course, feed my chickens, but that's like five minutes, tops. I don't gotta go to a pediatrics appointment or a soccer game. So I can sit on my butt and be lazy."

Josie is not happy with her current job but knows that if she were storytelling, it would be different. Josie shared:

"I don't think anybody wants to work... But, I wouldn't mind working if it was just talking and telling stories and writing stuff."

While Josie would love to follow her storytelling passion and maybe move back to Texas, she is just too tired to make progress:

"I don't have any kids to take care of, but I feel tired all the time. Just spending eight hours talking to people on the phone and having them tell me I'm the cause of all their problems, that's how customer service goes. And then I get home, and I don't want to deal with anything else. I just want to relax."

I asked Josie, "If your job is draining you that much, why do you keep going?" Her answer:

"Well, not starving is a good motivator. I like being able to buy food, I am looking for a different position, but so far, the only people that have replied to my request to be hired are scammers... It is so hard to get noticed by employers... They're preaching to us in the news that nobody wants to work. And then it's like, we can't even get a call back for the 12 jobs we've applied to."

Josie is applying to five jobs a week and is working hard to stay out of debt:

"I don't like to be in debt. I just don't like the concept of owing someone money. But, I understand that with credit scores, you need to get into debt to build up your credit score. So, I have done that before and then paid it off. I'm in debt right now because I had to have a dental procedure done a couple of months ago. But, I almost have that paid off."

Josie's retirement plans are simple:

"I hope that I make enough money on either the business or accounting to retire. That is as long as inflation doesn't force me to work 'til I die."

I asked her to describe her life in one word, and her answer was:

"Lost... I guess you just have all of your expectations for life. They just did not come about. You're told you're going to graduate high school, and you're going to get a big ceremony, and then you're going to go off to college, and you're going to get a degree and get a good job. Right. I just, I didn't follow any of that. So, I don't know what I'm supposed to do."

Josie got her GED and graduated early but did not get the ceremony or much else. She was in an abusive household and did not follow the "standard" script. Josie shared:

"I feel like, because I didn't follow the script that was hammered into me, I feel like I'm adrift."

Josie has been through a lot in her life. She is working hard to improve and find herself. She is trying to do better. I asked Josie if she saw the light at the end of the tunnel:

"I don't know if it's like a light at the end of the tunnel, but I am hopeful for the future. I think I'll improve myself and get a better job. I do think that construction business will take off."

Two months after the interview, Josie reached out to me and asked me to add this:

"I know it's been a while since I have done the interview, but some new information recently came to light that changes how I would have/already spent the inheritance I received from my father. Technically, my business partner embezzled $40K worth of the inheritance out of my account. This was $40K out of $110K, so it was a significant portion. However, we had already spent approximately $70K on a vehicle and various upgrades that would be necessary to use it as a working vehicle, and I had assumed the remaining amount had gone to purchasing tools. I was working full time and could barely function beyond going to work and coming home at the time, so I didn't question the amount spent on tools. And looking at credit reports would reveal that the remainder of the inheritance had been spent on tools. However, what the report would not show me, was that my business partner was returning all the tools purchased and getting refunds in cash.

He did this to pay for cancer treatments.

He had no insurance at the time (self-employed), and because we are not married, I could not add him to the insurance I have from my job. Suppose I had elected to spend the inheritance on a house or a down payment on a house (for creating room to have a child or other reasons). In that case, there is an astronomically high possibility that we would not have been able to afford the treatments. Feel free to imagine what the outcome of that would have been. He hid these treatments from everyone, including his long-term girlfriend. Thankfully, he only had stage I cancer, so full chemo was unnecessary, only chemo pills. Myself and his girlfriend did see him be very sick and assumed it was because he was studying too much. It turns out the opposite was true— he was studying to distract himself from the sickness. I do not fault my business partner in any way for doing this, and I am glad he was able to spend the money on the treatments before I invested the money into anything else.

I find it disgusting that in the 'land of the free', we need to use an accumulated lifetime of wealth from the deceased to keep the living alive."

15

KRISTI – A PORTRAIT OF FREEDOM AND PRACTICALITY

Kristi
38, Female, Married, Oklahoma
Master's in Education and Geology
Educator

K risti and her husband have applied an analytical approach to being Childfree and celebrate the freedom that resulted:

"We made a pros and cons list, and the cons side was way longer than the pros."

Kristi looks at the responsibility of having kids as "mental clutter":

"I think it [having kids] would be a big inconvenience in my life, both in terms of time and money and just like mental clutter. Having to keep track of who needs to go to the doctor when and daycare and, like, school conferences. I just don't feel like devoting that much energy and time to this other being, and it just seems like a simpler life to just worry about me and my husband and having fun and doing what we want to do."

It isn't that Kristi does not like kids. She works for a community college doing educational events with kids:

"I work at a community college, and I work with youth. K through eight is the bulk of what I do. It includes running a very large summer camp of about 250 kids for seven weeks. And then, during the school year, I partner with local districts helping with science education. I also work extensively with the Boy Scouts, and we offer merit badge classes through the college. I connect them with professors in the fields that match up with their merit badge classes and get them exposed to different career fields while they work on their badges."

Kristi and her husband value the freedom of being Childfree. They use that time to hike some fantastic national parks and playing board games is their hobby. In addition, they have the time to attend gaming conferences (like GenCon, they've gone 12 times) and connect with each other. One day, Kristi hopes to open a board game business and hold her own events:

"I like the fact that our life is very simple. I get up. I go to work, I work hard. I do a good job, but when I'm done with work, I'm done. I drive home, I eat dinner, and then I can just lounge out. We'll watch TV, and we'll burn through series on Netflix or Amazon. We'll lay on the couch and use Reddit until I'm tired. Then I go to bed. I don't have to worry about anybody else. No homework, bath time, storytime. It's just simple and easy. So, with additional free time, like on weekends, we'll have board game days with friends. We'll have game days at home. We'll cook really awesome food that we, you know, we can just devote our time to prepping and cooking without having to worry about children running around or needing diapers changed or anything else."

Kristi enjoys her Childfree life. I made her choose the most significant benefit of being Childfree:

"I would value time over money, but money is the second."

Kristi is in a good financial place. Her husband is a CERTIFIED FINANCIAL PLANNER™. They have a plan for retirement in their mid-40s. Being Childfree allows them to take amazing vacations. They are in a financial situation that may be enviable to many. Yet it is time that is the most significant benefit—the time (and freedom) to do what they want:

"I envisioned what my life would be like if I had a kid. My brother has children, and he has young kids, a five-year-old and a one-year-old. And I know that when he comes home from work, it's getting dinner ready. It's trying to play with his kids in the little time they have before you start bath time, bedtime, storytime thing. And then by the time they're in bed, he, you know, he's tired from working. So, he might have, you know, an hour or so to himself. I want more than that. I want hours to myself. I don't want to have to worry about anyone else."

To Kristi, it isn't all bad having kids. They can provide a sense of purpose (at a cost):

"I can see why people have kids because it kind of gives you the sense of purpose. Right. And that makes sense to me, but we've still both firmly decided that it's not that the sense of purpose isn't worth the hassle of actually having children and what that means. So, okay, fine. We have a sense of purpose, but we've lost everything else. Right? We've lost our freedom. We've lost a huge chunk of our money. We've lost our free time. And that just seems really sad."

Does Kristi have any regrets about being Childfree?:

"Never once."

Kristi is a self-proclaimed "money nerd." She has always been a saver and had an IRA at 14. Throughout her life, she had a plan to retire early. You would think that her husband being a CFP® professional rubbed off on her, but it was the other way around. Her husband was a paleontologist and needed a career change. He got interested in the stock market, and in Kristi's words:

"He was like, I get it. Now we need to double down and make this early retirement thing a reality."

Kristi has always been practical. She grew up on a farm, and everything had a purpose:

"I was raised on a farm, and we didn't have animals that didn't serve a purpose. Right? We couldn't have horses because you can't eat a horse. We could have cows and chickens because you can eat them. Right. They serve a purpose. The cats served a purpose because they caught the mice. Our dog served a purpose because he was used for hunting, but it wasn't a pet dog. It was a hunting dog. So, I think that's been drilled into my mind. Things need to have a purpose."

Kristi has a list for everything. She has been on some fantastic adventures, including climbing mountains and seeing glaciers that you and I may only see in a book. While her husband may be more spontaneous, he allows Kristi to plan everything. So when I challenged her with Kinder's life questions, and she only had five to 10 years to live, she just made a list:

"If I knew I had five to 10 years, I would assume the worst-case scenario and assume five years. So, I think I would pick the top five favorite places in the world that I wanted to visit either for the first time or were to see again. And I would make that a priority for the next five years. And then, after that, I would look at each year as a bonus year. So I would extend my list. Year six would be bonus year number one, bonus your number two, et cetera."

Even her hiking and vacation has a practical purpose:

"I've gotten a lot out of our hiking trips, and it's not just the cool glacier that we got to walk on or the 14-mile hike to the Burgess shale to see the fossils. I feel like there's a lot more that I get out of hiking than just that. A lot of it is the reinforcement of the mental stick-to-it-ness because climbing a mountain for seven miles uphill is hard, and your feet hurt and you're tired, and your pack is heavy, but you have to finish it. Right. You started it. And there's a reason not to finish it. The weather isn't stopping you. The only thing that would stop you is mental weakness. But you recognize that, like when you get to the top, you still have to walk back out seven miles. So, there's like, you're only almost to the halfway point, and it's okay that you're tired, but you have to keep going. So that kind of thinking applies to other hard things in my life... I think putting myself in situations that are difficult, like both mentally and physically, is good."

Kristi's practical approach to life seems almost like stoicism (my word, not hers). She has a plan and is ready for anything that happens. This was most obvious when Kristi attacked the questions about "who will take care of you when you are older." Her answer is no one. She is going to "opt-out":

"I feel like if I got into a situation where I'm like 77, and I don't have enough money anymore, it's pretty easy to just opt out on life and, you know, see ya. No one's gonna miss me. Right? So, we've talked about that. Like opting out together, just being like, all right, we've done this thing. Like, we've done everything we wanted to do. We're out of money. So, we're just gonna zip on out. And, and there's certainly no, there's no one that's impacted by that. The chances are that my brother will also be gone at that point. And no one's affected by it."

Kristi is only 38, yet she has already achieved her educational and professional goals, along with many of her life goals. She has a Bachelor's and two Master's degrees. She enjoys her work (for the most part), and she is working on her goal to see more of the planet (she was an earth science major, so it fits). Her only other goal is:

"Just to be like a decent person and live a life that I'm proud of. I don't want to be 87 and be like, oh crap. I was such a jerk."

Even once she passes, Kristi has a plan. Kristi and her husband have already decided to make an impact in their estate plan:

"A third of our money will go toward the Glacier National Park Conservancy. A third of our money will go to the Grand Teton National Park Conservancy. And just as a fail-safe in case something really crazy happened and both of those national parks were gone. The other third and/or the rest would go toward the National Park Foundation."

I consider myself a rather practical person, but Kristi has me beat. She has managed to give everything a purpose to gain time, money, and the freedom to do what they want. She is living her own best, authentic life. And now she is sharing that life with others:

"I think more and more people are recognizing that you don't have to have kids. I encounter little girls all the time at work that see my ring, and they ask if I'm married. Then their next question is, oh, so you also have kids then? And when I tell them, no, I don't, and they're very confused. And they'll say, like, I thought you were married. I am.

But that doesn't mean that you'll have to have kids. And it's like, I blew their mind. And they're like, but when you're married, you have kids. So, no, you don't all. Some people don't.

I feel like more and more people are recognizing that you can choose. It doesn't have to go hand in hand (kids and marriage), and it's a big responsibility. And it's something that should be thought through very carefully, not jumped into impulsively because it literally will change your life, maybe for the worse. So I think encouraging people to think about big decisions like that is important."

16

KRISTINA – A PORTRAIT OF A
CAT LADY

Kristina
39, Female, Single, Asexual, Washington
Bachelor's in Aeronautical Engineering
Aerodynamic Performance Engineer

Kristina is a self-declared "cat lady, spinster, rocket scientist." She is 39 and shares her life with three black cats in the Pacific Northwest. She is an avid reader and loves sending postcards to her niblings (nieces and nephews) and others. She is asexual, single and not looking, and happy with her life. Kristina is an aerospace engineer and happily Childfree.

Kristina shared why she decided to be Childfree:

"I came to that conclusion around age eight. I looked around, and it was like, you know, I hate children. I have not liked being around children since I was a child, and it's not changed since that. I like my niblings in small doses, and mostly I send them postcards... I can't even consistently get myself dinner regularly, much less, you know, care and feeding for a small being that depends on you for everything. So, I just decided it was not for me. I've gotten no pushback from any person I know, familial or otherwise. So either they came to the conclusion that [she should be Childfree] the same way I came to the conclusion or they sort of decided it would be a terrible idea. Or maybe they're just like: well, that's your decision."

Kristina sees the most significant benefit of being Childfree to be the time it gives her:

"Free time. I mean, other than your various job things and various chore things that are non-optional, basically, you have time. I also come from this as a person who is single and not looking. So I can do whatever I want with this time that is not taken up by other things. And there is no one to be like, you have to do this or this critical thing that will come by with drastic consequences if you don't do it. The only things that are affected by that are me and my cats. And I'm pretty good at keeping the cats alive. I'm somewhat less good at keeping myself in good health, but that's a little more complicated. And just the mental burden of children is not something I think I'll ever be able to deal with."

Kristina uses her time for her interests, including being an avid reader:

"I use it [her time] for a lot of reading. I am a big fan fiction fan of various sorts. I read a lot. Not all of it's published, some of it is just stories online, but I read a lot. I sometimes cross-stitch. I talk to friends. So I mean, just stuff that fills life. I'm not curing cancer or anything, but it's good enough for me. I'm not one of those people who are, like, requiring their 15 minutes of fame in Wikipedia or whatever, to be important. There's a very low chance that I will ever be important enough to anyone to be mentioned anywhere. So that's fine."

Kristina has been reading since she was young, and it hasn't stopped. When she isn't reading, she is taking care of her cats, collecting teapots (including many spectacularly tacky ones), or working on her list of 100 goals:

> "There's a hundred of them [goals], including being debt-free at one point. Being able to retire with at least a hundred grand a year. Being able to have a house with a 'catio,' which is like a cat patio outside. Visiting my family. Learn archery. Learn various languages..."

Kristina loves bullet journaling (which helps with her ADHD) and picked up the 100 goal habit from a recently-read self-help book. I asked her how she prioritizes these goals, as it seemed like a lot to me:

> "They aren't prioritized except by how much effort I'm putting into any one of them at any given time, which for the most part is zero at the moment... So a lot of them aren't even terribly important goals or even really big goals."

Kristina doesn't want to rank her goals, and she is okay if she does not achieve them all. In some ways, the list may be more like a bucket list, but without the deadline at the end:

> "It's probably more like a bucket list than anything else. And it took me years to make the list. For most people, you run out of things to do before you hit a hundred. They're like, what else could I do with my life? I can't think of anything else. Sometimes it takes a few years to even come up with a hundred things. Unlike a bucket list, which is just, you know, stuff I should do before I die, the imminent feature, there are probably more long-term goals on the list."

I asked Kristina what gets in the way of achieving her goals, and she shared:

> "Mostly mental health issues. I have chronic depression that comes and goes."

Kristina is not alone. Depression and ADHD are very common, and it was part of her reasoning for being Childfree:

"To be honest, it's a very difficult disease to manage, especially with not a lot of family nearby to sort of pick up the slack. It's also something I would never want to pass on to children. Based on my family history, it is genetic for me to like three grandparents. This is not something horrible that happened to me. It's just, you know, your brain hates you."

Kristina would love to visit her family more (although COVID-19 has not made that easy). She might even live closer to them if there were jobs, but her career is very specialized. Financially, Kristina's goal is to reduce her debt load. She is saving for retirement, and her condo's value is doing well, but paying down her debt has been a challenge. Nevertheless, she keeps trying to focus on it, maybe for the next two years:

"Let's just focus on these next few years. And then the next year comes, and oh, well, here's a mental health crisis. That will shit on everything. So let's, you know, take six steps back. And now we're four years from getting out of debt. So let's restart from there."

Balancing finances while going through a health crisis can be extremely hard. Medical bills are the top reason for bankruptcies in the U.S., but that does not even account for missed work and the ancillary effects. Making progress on your financial goals sometimes takes a little bit of luck (or a bit more, as Kristina shares):

"It's a little more than a little bit of luck. It requires you to be in good physical and mental health for long periods, which is not something that everyone can do. And it is not something that they have any control over."

Kristina plans to retire at age 67 and with $4 million in her retirement plan. She shared her retirement plans:

> "I will send a lot of postcards. I will save a lot of cats. I'm hopefully going to end up in some sort of, like, 'Golden Girls' retirement place. I will have a bunch of my old lady friends, and we all live in a house together and have good times."

Kristina has her long-term care plans set. She lives in Washington, and everyone in the state is either required to have long-term care insurance, or they will be opted-in to the state long-term care plan (and pay a tax for it). Kristina stated it this way:

> "Either you do it [buy long-term care insurance], or the state government will do it for you, and they will do it in a much shittier fashion. So just do it... It's actually really difficult to get long-term care insurance under the age of 40. No one wants to talk to you because they don't believe you will pay for it for the next 40 years or whatever. So I got it on a special dispensation. Under normal circumstances, unless you're like 50 or 60 years old, the people who give out long-term care insurance won't even talk to you."

Kristina wouldn't change much about her life. She controls her life and has made choices to make it better over time. She is happy with her cats, reading, and living for herself:

> "I understand that people do things that they don't want to do. But, if your life is just full of all the things you hate doing, and you have the power to change things, you probably should. Otherwise, you're going to look back when you're 70 years old and go, I hated everything I did during the course of my life."

17

LAURA – A PORTRAIT OF STABILITY

Laura
31, Female, Married, Wisconsin
Master's in Nonprofit Management
Finance

L aura is married and works in finance. She is passionate about her causes and making an impact on the world. However, she balances her passions with a need for stability. Her need for stability and avoiding financial insolvency drive many of her decisions. Like many people, she is trying to find a sweet spot between making the right financial decisions and the right decisions for her heart (and the world).

Laura never wanted children:

"I think I've known since I was a child that I didn't have an interest in being a parent. That just remained as I got older. Then I met somebody in the same boat who never had an interest in having children. I kind of wondered if that would change as I got older. As I entered my thirties, I had this realization that it was never going to change, and I was always going to remain Childfree. I just never felt compelled to be a parent or have a child or to bring somebody else into this world."

Laura values the freedom and flexibility of being Childfree:

"For me, it's the freedom and flexibility in your life to be able to change and grow and evolve without having this extra baggage of another human being. For me, that's been a huge benefit because I like moving around the country. I like traveling. I like changing my career. I like doing different things at the time in my life that suits me. It's really difficult when you are responsible for another human being so fully to be able to continue to evolve and change and change your life."

Laura provided an example of how she has used this freedom and flexibility in her life:

"About two and a half years ago, I was in a place in my career, working in a nonprofit, where I was a little burnt out, and I just realized I wanted to take a sabbatical. So I actually quit my job and didn't work for three months, which is the exact amount of time I planned for. It was wonderful. I had time to recharge and think about what I wanted. I moved to a different city during that time. It was this really freeing moment for me. I don't think I would have been able to do that if I was responsible for feeding and housing another individual."

Laura does not have any regrets from being Childfree:

"No regrets. Sometimes I wonder about missing out on this very profound life experience. I know a lot of people who are having children right now, and it does seem like a very loving, exciting, very rich part of their lives. Sometimes I wonder how I'll feel about that when I'm older if I feel as if I've missed out on something very profound... I think for me, I'm willing to take that risk of missing out. I'd rather regret not having children than to have children and regret it. I think that would be much more serious. I mean, I know people who have had children and regretted it, and I feel like that is the worst option."

Laura has a deep passion for conservation, the environment, various causes, and helping others. But, as she shares:

"I've always had this image of, like, building a dream home, cultivating land, spending more time doing, like, impactful, meaningful work."

So why hasn't Laura achieved her goal yet?:

"I think the constraints of life prevent me from doing a lot of those things. It could be time management. A lot of daily life demands so much of your time and attention. There are many demands on my time like my job, maintaining my home, maintaining my relationships, maintaining my physical health on top of everything. There's so much that distracts away from attaining our goals. It's very easy to get caught up in daily life, which makes it very hard to find those moments where you can work on things that fulfill you... I think it's up to me at this point to figure out exactly how I can structure my time to achieve those things that I've always dreamed of. "

In addition to time, it may be finances that hold her back:

"I do think that cultivating enough financial wealth for myself right now is a part of what holds me back from achieving those things and having more time to devote to those things. So it feels like at this point in my life, it's a must that I have to put in the time [towards finances]."

Part of the reason Laura works so hard at finances is to prepare for her future (especially her elder years). Childfree individuals know they need to provide for their future as they don't have kids. Census data says that in adults over 55 in the U.S. who are childless, 2.5% receive financial support from family. Interestingly, in the same sample, only 1.5% of parents receive financial support from family. So Laura is looking at her future and planning to take care of herself as everyone should:

> "I think part of my motivation is that I feel there is a little bit of a risk in the future. I won't have people to support me quite as much as some other people would have if they had children, but that's never a guarantee. So, right now, I feel compelled to work as much as I need to, to be able to support myself as I continue to grow older."

I asked Laura if there is a "magic number" at which she would feel like she has enough money to feel safe and follow her dreams:

> "I don't have a magic number. I mean, if I had enough in retirement investments to maintain the same standard of living I have now, I would be happy. For me, that would probably be a minimum of $2 million in investments. I would love to say less, but considering inflation and how expensive living is becoming, I don't know that it could be less than that. I think $2 million would probably be very much the threshold. If I was able to achieve that level of investment, like, tomorrow at this age, I could make it work. It would be enough to sustain me if I was careful with how I manage that money."

Laura doesn't really consider herself a FIRE person. She is just trying to ensure she has enough finances to be safe and stable. Both Laura and her husband work. He loves what he does, but Laura seems a bit restless. Laura wants to make a more significant impact and achieve more. They both effectively earn the same salary, and they could live on just one salary. So then why doesn't Laura quit her current job and follow her dreams?:

"That's a good question. I feel like there are just things that keep getting in the way. I don't know if it's a time management issue for us. I think there's this assumption that when you're Childfree, you have significantly more time than other people... In our own individual lives, regardless of whether you have children or not, you're always going to find reasons or issues not to do what you say you are going to do... You don't have that excuse when you don't have kids, but you can still find excuses. Like you can still find reasons not to do the things you're gonna say you're going to do."

Being Childfree almost gives us too many options at times. The flexibility of being Childfree allows us to make different decisions than those with kids, but at the same time, it puts pressure on us. Laura explains well how we can find ways to fill our time and put roadblocks in our way. It becomes a real challenge when we are unhappy with our work (or another part of our lives). Laura is okay with what she is doing for a living but wants to do more for the world. She wants to make an impact. Her work is sucking the energy out of her so that she does not have the energy to do the things she wants to do. So why keep doing it?:

"There's a sense of stability that I get out of it. I don't hate it by any means. The people I work with are lovely. It's a very stable job that feels doable. And I like the people I work with, but no joy is not a part of it... You know, now that you mentioned it, I think it's fear-based. What I mean by that is when I look at how things are just like, like economically in this country, I have a lot of fear around not having money and a lot of fear around being financially unstable. We don't live in a country where we are privileged enough that if we get sick, there's a guarantee we're going to get healthcare. That terrifies me. I've known several people in my personal life who've been in that situation. So, it's not something that I can conceptualize. I can conceptualize being sick and then being indebted the rest of my life for getting cancer or something, which terrifies me. It terrifies me the idea of living becoming so expensive that I would then have a very substandard quality of life because I didn't have enough money. So, it's sad to say, but it is for fear-based reasons that I do what I do and I just don't ever want to be in a situation where I am not financially solvent. I've seen it happen to people, and it's just, it's no way to live."

This fear of not having money (especially regarding healthcare costs) is widespread. I have some of this myself. In my other interviews, money fears were often tied to growing up poor. However, that wasn't the case for Laura:

"I guess my parents would probably be considered upper-middle-class. They were very vague about how much our household income was. I think one time I saw our income tax returns, and it was somewhere between $200,000 and $300,000 in like household income, which I guess was upper-middle-class. However, the way my parents managed money made me feel like we didn't have that much money. They were very weird about it. They were constantly stressed about money, yet we lived in a nice place. They were constantly stressed about money, yet they could pay for our college. So, growing up, it was confusing. I didn't quite understand where we stood financially."

The way we were raised with money has a significant impact on our relationship with money throughout our life. The challenge is that having more money does not necessarily make us feel more secure or stable. Laura stated that her goal is $2 million, and she should reach that without a problem. She has enough invested now that she should be fine, given time and average returns. But yet she worries:

"I've looked at what we have in investments and how much we're contributing monthly. I know we're fine. If we worked until we were 65, we would probably have enough money to pay for the college tuition of every single one of our nephews and nieces and retire. I think it stems from my childhood. I just grew up in a place where it was just like, money was stress. And it just felt like there was never enough. I think we were technically like, okay and well above the median household income, but it was just this feeling of just like, oh, we'll never have enough. And like, well, what if we need more?"

I spent some time with Laura looking at her finances. She's in a good spot both for now and the future. But, even though she is in a good spot, Laura keeps working on improving her finances. She is making a conscious choice (as many of us do) to put her finances ahead of her dreams. In the end, I asked her if she was okay with that decision?:

"Am I okay with it? No, I'm not okay with it. This is something I've been thinking about for a long time. How can I get my life to a point where I feel comfortable? It's something that my husband and I have talked about a lot. Like, do we want to buy a very cheap house somewhere and just bring our living costs down as little as possible to focus on the things we want to do and do them now? And is that achievable, and is it something we should just do? I don't think I'm okay right now with the way things are. It's probably why we've moved a couple of times. It's probably why I've changed careers a couple of times. I think I am looking for something. I think I'm looking for that spot in my life to be able to do those things that I want to do. Why haven't I found that spot? I don't know. I think it comes back to this fear, this anxiety about being unstable, being financially insolvent."

So what does the future hold for Laura and her husband?:

"I'm at a very strange crossroads in my life. I'm trying to figure out when is it time to take that plunge and live my life the way I want to live? And I do feel like, for whatever reason, I continue to talk myself out of it. I talk myself out of making a big change in my life that would allow me to do those things. I know that I cannot continue

doing that for much longer. I am turning 32 next month. I don't want
to lead a life that feels unfulfilling. I don't want to be older and look
back on my life and think, why was I so afraid not to do that job?
What I'm saying is I feel like I'm getting to a point very soon where I
think things are going to have to change. I don't honestly know how
much longer I want to continue doing things the way I've been
doing them."

18

LORNA – A PORTRAIT OF ACCIDENTAL FIRE

Lorna
52 years old, Female, Widowed, Massachusetts
Master's in Computer Science
Retired

L orna came to the U.S. from Scotland approximately 25 years ago. She has gone from growing up in the lower working class to retiring last year at age 51. She has faced multiple sclerosis and lost her wife, and yet still achieved great things in that time. She is Childfree, stayed out of debt, invested early, and is living her best life. She did not follow a complex financial plan but just did the right things at each turn. Lorna is a portrait of "accidental" FIRE (Financial Independence, Retire Early).

Lorna did not make a big decision to be Childfree:

"I didn't decide. I never had any desire for children growing up. My relatives were always like, 'oh, it will change when you get married.' So I was like, let me see... Nope. Then when I discovered that I was gay, I was like, well, that makes it even easier. Doesn't it?"

Lorna sees freedom as the most significant benefit to being Childfree:

"Just the freedom to, to spend doing what you want when you want. You get to focus on yourself. I read the Pope's article the other day about how we're all selfish. And I was like, yes, coming from you [the Pope] who's Childfree, but okay. I mean, you do get to be selfish."

Lorna also sees the financial benefits of being Childfree. She looks at her friends and sees how much they spend on school and sports and can't help but see the financial impact. Then again, it is different now than when she was raised in Scotland. In comparison to parents traveling all the time to see games and tournaments. Lorna shared:

"I think my Mum came to my sports day at school once in my entire time at school."

Being Childfree has allowed Lorna to be financially free, but she still worries:

"I am financially free now, but there's that weight [finances] at the back of my mind. I look at the net worth statement, then I'm like, hmm, but what if it just goes to zero tomorrow for some reason?"

Lorna would love to upgrade from her Kia Sportage to a BMW or Jaguar, but she is very practical:

"A car is a depreciating asset. As much as I like cars, at the end of the day, after the first couple of months that you've had it, it's just a car."

At some point, Lorna will move back to Scotland to be with her family but may end up splitting her time between the U.S. and Scotland. Her dog (a boxer/beagle mix) is keeping her here now, but also, it is just nicer weather here and not always gray.

"I've been here 25 years now, and when I go back to visit [Scotland], it's nice. But can I deal with the gray sky all the time? I didn't realize how depressing it was until I came here. I was driving to work every day, and the blue sky and blue water made me happy."

It is not a question of if Lorna moves back, but when:

"I definitely want to get back there [Scotland] before I'm 70 just because I'm not impressed with the healthcare over here [in the U.S.]."

Healthcare is important to Lorna. She was diagnosed with multiple sclerosis (MS) at age 27, before she transferred to the U.S., and that has shaped her life in many ways:

"When I was 27, I was diagnosed with MS. And that was a big thing for me. But, they [doctors] can't predict what it's going to be like. So, you don't know. I might be in a wheelchair in five years' time. So, you pretty much try to do as much as you can when you can."

Lorna would love to get a big motorcycle:

"None of that Harley-Davidson crap, I want a Japanese ZXR."

However, she is practical to the core, and practicality wins in most cases. One of her fears or anxieties in retirement is that she may become too cheap with herself. She worries about running out of money and being too frugal when there is no need to be:

"So it's like I have to push myself not to be quite practical all the time."

I did push her a bit and ask about what her last "non-practical" spending was, but she couldn't think of anything off the top of her head (but that may be due to COVID-19). The last thing she did for fun was going to a movie theater.

Lorna didn't have a plan to retire early. She did not enjoy work and did not like the stress. Lorna looks at it this way:

> "I'm 52 and retired last year at 51. I was like, okay, I've saved enough money. And this should last me the rest of my life as long as no comets are hitting the ground... I do want to do something more. I didn't want to have that work stress. But at the same time, I was like, well, I'm retired, and I can always volunteer. But I don't want to be tied down to go somewhere every week. There are almost too many choices now."

When Lorna first went to a financial advisor, she was told she might be able to retire at 55, and she was excited, but that was 20 years ago. When she got married and went to an advisor together with her wife, it was a different picture:

> "I got married, and my wife was, she was a little older than me. She was nine years older. But she was the same as me. She came from a poor background, and she was a saver as well. So when we finally went to a financial advisor where we did our money jointly, we were surprised and like, whoa, we're rich!"

There was a big disconnect between Lorna and her wife on when to retire. Her wife wanted to retire at 70, and Lorna was looking more at 50. Lorna suggested that her wife could keep working until 70 to get health insurance, but that did not work out. Lorna lost her wife three years ago, days before her 60th birthday. Losing her wife helped Lorna look at work differently:

> "I was like, this is all pointless, this working stuff. I did think it was funny that your whole life someone's told you; It's time to go to school. It's time to get a job. It's time to go up the ladder. But there's

nobody that comes along and says, it's time to retire. So I discovered the FIRE movement and figured it out for myself. But then I had to run the numbers by someone else. 'Cause I was like, is this some hocus-pocus, or is this real?"

Lorna's largest hesitation in moving to retirement was health insurance. So she did a bit of research on those who have done FIRE and what they do for insurance. Lorna found that she could be on an ACA (Affordable Care Act) plan and that she could retire:

"Especially with the MS. I know I'm on meds that are expensive. And then I have my neurologist, and I have to get MRIs. Those aren't cheap if you don't have insurance. I just looked at the statement of benefits for my plan. I had some MRIs that would have cost me $5,000, but then the insurance knocked that down well over half. So in the end, I have a $15 copay, YEAH!"

Lorna has been doing well and hasn't had a flare-up in over 10 years. She focuses on her health in her retirement:

"I have learned to cook healthy meals. I joined the gym. I have a personal trainer, and I work out in one form or another every day. The dog enjoys it because he goes for more walks."

Lorna is also learning more about investing and taxes. Although she is trying not to worry about her finances as much:

"I'm trying to stop looking at the stock market every day. I've got enough cash to do me a good few years now. So I don't need to worry about what's going on in the stock market."

Lorna's financial plan wasn't much of a plan and was definitely not a FIRE plan. It was more a reflection of how she grew up and wanted things to be different. As Lorna puts it, her mom was a single mom "before it became almost trendy", and they struggled. Growing up, it was evident that they were very working class. The kids on the other side of the road lived in a new development and had new bikes. Lorna's bike got her where she needed to go, but it wasn't anything fancy or new. Lorna shared:

> "I worked from the age of 15 at part-time jobs. Our household income was so low that the government paid for my college tuition and travel expenses."

Watching her mom struggle with a low-income job, loans, and trying to avoid debt, helped shape Lorna:

> "I didn't want a 'woman's job' because I could see nurses, teachers, secretaries, they didn't get paid a lot. Men got paid much more money. Like engineers, executives, they get big salaries. I was like, okay, I want to be an engineer because that's where the money is... It was funny; they were doing a push for women into engineering when I left school. So I studied electronic engineering. And I was the only girl in the whole year at the college. I switched to IT courses after a couple of years, and there were more females in classes then."

The one thing Lorna always knew she wanted financially was no debt:

> "I never really wanted debt... I came over to the U.S. with two bags and about $10,000 of debt. And the first year, I paid off that $10,000 debt. I had saved up enough money to buy out the car lease. I was debt-free, YEAH! Then I saved what was my lease payment so that with my next car, I could buy it in cash."

Besides having a mortgage for some time, Lorna has been debt-free for the past 25 years. When she first transferred to the U.S., they told her about a 401(k) account, and she wasn't interested. Lorna became interested when she heard there was free money with it (the employer match), which introduced her to the stock market. She reflects that many of her friends in the U.K. are not investing, as it is not something they are exposed to. Lorna then went on to see Suze Orman talking on PBS about Roth IRAs, and that also sounded like a good idea. At her core, Lorna is a saver:

"I was always very aware of lifestyle inflation. When I first came over, I rented rooms and stuff, and that's fine. I was more than happy to deprive myself of some of the luxuries if it meant that I could save and have stability."

Lorna was saving more for stability than for retirement:

"I guess MS forced me [to focus on stability] in some ways. I didn't know how long I might be able to work. So it was like, okay, save as much as you can because you just don't know. I could have a flare-up and might end up in a wheelchair or might lose my eyesight or something, but it never happened. I remember when I first got diagnosed, and the HR woman at work in England said, 'you know, you can go on disability.' So then I looked into disability work benefits, and I was like, ugh. And then I looked at disabled housing, and I was like, oh my God, this is just depressing. It was just that, like, there was no future. So yeah. I was run, run, in the other direction as fast as you can."

I asked Lorna what Childfree Wealth means to her:

"It means estate planning is a hell of a lot harder. It also means there's no part of it that is about leaving a legacy or having to help out the grandkids or any of that."

Lorna wants to give her money to people who need it but is still working on her charitable giving. She does not see herself like Oprah giving to everyone or like "real rich people" giving away money. Right now, Lorna just doesn't see herself as rich (even though, by many measures, she is). Lorna dreams about maybe just giving her money to a friendly cashier helping her at the store, and I'm not going to be surprised if she does.

19

MAGGIE – A PORTRAIT OF STRENGTH

Maggie
47, Female, Widowed, Washington, DC
Master's Degree in Political Science
Diplomat

M aggie is a portrait of strength. She was raised by a single mom and grew up poor. The result of growing up poor is that as she says:

"I'm terrified of poverty. ...I have a fear of being poor... I had a mother who made $30,000 a year raising two children and lived check to check. Like, you know mac and cheese was our dinner...."

Maggie is not alone. The way you were raised often shapes your relationship with money. For Maggie, it has created a set of bookends. Not only did growing up poor shape her relationships with money, but it shaped her picture of Childfree Wealth. When asked what Childfree Wealth means to her, her answer was simple:

"I'm not living the adult life my mother led."

It isn't that Maggie has something against her mother. As we talked, it became apparent how much she loves and cares for her mother. She plans to take care of both her mother and stepfather as they age (currently they are 75 and 73). Maggie bought a house bigger than she needed with a plan that they could both move in with her if needed. The reality is that she has been caring for her mother since she was age 10 or so. Even as a child, Maggie helped her mom find a balance with her emotions around finances and relationships. Maggie wants stability in her life that she did not have as a child, and her mom didn't have until much later in life when she met Maggie's stepdad.

The challenge of growing up poor and supporting her mother from a young age has shaped Maggie. As a result, Maggie freely admits:

"I have control issues."

When reflecting on her childhood and her mom, Maggie shared:

"I saw her as having very little control over her life, whether it was financially, emotionally, or with what she did with her time. Her emotions almost ran out of control because she was pulled in so many different directions. I just saw that. And I went, that can't be me."

Control was a large part of why Maggie chose to be Childfree:

"You just lose a lot of control when you have a child. It's your time, or in some ways, it's your autonomy. I enjoy being me. I see a lot of people first identify themselves as a parent, as opposed to an individual. I think it's a benefit that I can actually say who I am as a person before I'm anything else."

Maggie did not make this decision alone:

"I was married for about 18 years, and my husband passed away about five years ago... We made the decision fairly early on not to have kids... When I met my spouse, we were both very much on the fence about it. I always felt like if one of us felt super strongly about it, then we might've changed our minds. But since we were both kinda like ehhh [*shrug*]... It's an important thing. It's one of those decisions that needs to be two yeses, or it's a no."

Maggie and her spouse were together for 18 years before he passed at 50. But, like many Childfree couples, they were never legally married (32.1% of childless individuals in the US over 55 were never married). Maggie explains:

"I call him my husband, but we never got married. We were together for 18 years. We owned a home together. We had shared finances. We never got married for a number of reasons. Not wanting kids was a big factor. We said well, if we wanted kids, then we would have gotten married."

Losing her husband has given Maggie a different perspective. Beyond the personal loss impact, it has shaped how she looks at her past and future. For example, in explaining why she sometimes holds herself back from her dreams, Maggie shared that healthcare costs were one piece and also that:

"...the other piece is knowing that all the pressure is on me, right? There's no fallback income. I didn't realize how much that shaped my thinking until we did go through a rough patch. My husband had his own real estate company, still based in our hometown. And, he almost had no money for a year or two after a hurricane. The hurricane wiped out everything, I was supporting us. I wasn't very senior in my job, and I was like, oh God, this is hard with one income. My income has probably doubled since that time, but the flip side is that it's also just my income. And so those two things kind of make me nervous."

Maggie has achieved great things in life, has a great income now, but still struggles for control. Maggie has overcome significant challenges and is a great planner, but she is still a control freak. Being Childfree helped her to have control over her life yet allows for flexibility that can be paralyzing at times.

Does Maggie have any regrets about being Childfree?:

"I've never really, I've never regretted the choice of being Childfree. There were times, particularly right after my husband died, when having a kid would have been a really nice anchor because it would have been something you could focus on. And it gave you, like, routine, right? 'Cause you know, you have to get up every day, and you have to feed, you have to clothe. You have to do whatever it is you have to do depending on the age of the child. Right. And so after he passed, there were moments where I was like, man, if we had a kid, at least I would have [that routine]... But then after I kind of got over that hill, and I realized, oh wait, then I would be doing this all by myself. I'd be a single parent. That's not something I ever wanted in my life. ...[being Childfree] is something that constantly changes that flexibility versus freedom kind of, depending on where you're at in the moment. It is freeing, but it's also scary. Freeing [for Maggie] is when you don't have kids. And then also like when you find yourself suddenly single, decision-making can become very difficult because you don't [have anyone else]. You're the only calculus, and sometimes you feel like your decisions are very selfish because it's based on what you just want as a person. ... And it can be a little overwhelming. That being said, I'm still okay with that."

Maggie is at a point in her life where she needs to make some decisions. She is coming up on 20 years of service with the government and needs to choose when to retire (with a government pension). She's done great financially and could probably retire just off her net worth of over $1.5 million. While she says she has a dream to open a great wine bar on a beach, her retirement plans are more subdued and reflect finding a balance and the fear of being poor. I asked her what number she would have to have in the bank to get over this fear, and Maggie shared:

> "I don't know, frankly. ...My cousin [who is also Childfree] and I actually talked about this a lot. I'm probably a little bit better off [as a whole] than she is, but we're in the same place in life, and we were talking about this, and we're not sure if there's ever the right number that takes away that fear."

As with all my interviews, I asked Maggie the three Kinder Questions. As we went through the questions, Maggie had a physical reaction to the second question, which encouraged her to think about if she only had five or 10 years to live. Her face lit up. She perked up as if a weight had been lifted off her shoulders. It was then that she seemed to get over the fear of being poor and became able to dream about a life that was truly hers:

> "I would cash everything out. I would buy myself a nice little house, probably not little, a nice house on a beach or near a beach. Um, and I would just do whatever the 'F' I wanted. If I wanted to get on a plane and go to Bali, I'd go. I'd probably, you know, help my best friend's daughter. Who's very young. She's my beneficiary of everything. I'd probably go ahead and give some money to her to make sure, you know, she's got what she needs, but for the most part, I would just make it all 'F-you' money."

The change was remarkable to me. It shows the power of our past and existing mental models on our decisions every day. Maggie has done a great job saving, planning, and counting the dollars. She has an Excel spreadsheet she regularly checks, has worked with a financial advisor, and done many of the "right" things towards FIRE (Financial Independence, Retire Early). Retirement is a real option for her. Yet she struggles:

"I did a lot of therapy [after my husband passed], and I know all this goes back to the two sides of your brain. You have the rational side and the more emotional side. And I, for the most part, let the rational side dictate. And then there are certain things that just like emotionally, just override."

Maggie is not unique here. So much of our success and happiness with finances are tied to our behaviors and emotions. So many of us believe that if we hit a certain number, everything will magically be perfect, but that just isn't the case. The numbers don't drive things. Our emotions do. The result for Maggie is a dichotomy in her decision-making process:

"I either overthink, and I am slow and steady, or I just go all in, and I don't think about it. I have ideas, and that's it. When I bought my house in my hometown, I walked into the house and said, I love this house. I'm buying it. This is my investment. I'm doing this. I bought it. I didn't even think about it overnight. Right. Yet, I mulled over a $10,000 fix to my deck. Right. And it's just, and I know, I know this is my behavior."

Yet now Maggie has to decide if she will make the leap to retirement. She has done very well. She started as a middle range (GS-8) employee in the government and now is at the highest rank of the government pay schedule (GS-15). She has a job she seems to enjoy. Maggie has done things in her career that some people can only dream of:

"My cousin is in the same boat. We are the first women in our family that went to college. We're the first women that made over a hundred thousand dollars a year. We're both pushing close to $200K a year, which is a major success. And you don't want to tie your success to money, but it's hard thinking about walking away from that kind of money. I know if I stayed with the government for my full 30 years, I would be making more in retirement than I do right now. And it is hard to wrap my mind around walking away from something like that. After seeing a mother that made 30 grand a year, right? Or just seeing how many other women struggle to break these glass ceilings. And here I am, you know, a woman. I became a GS-15 in the government at 38. I did it in less than ten years. It is a pretty amazing timeframe to have done that in... I just look at myself, and I'm like, you know, I worked hard to get here. Is it okay to walk away from that for less and just live on a lot less money?"

It becomes a debate about what you want your life to look like. Maggie is at a crossroads and is doing all of this while planning to care for her elderly parents. She bought a house with room for them, and in Washington DC, where there are excellent elder care options:

"I was like, well, if I'm going to be potentially on the hook [to care for her parents], I might as well live somewhere where I can get the social services. So I'm okay with it. I, you know, I, sometimes I bitch about it, but, you know, I wouldn't have agreed to it if I wasn't okay with it."

Unsurprisingly, Maggie set conditions on this care plan:

"I have to have full medical and financial control if you want me to do this. All the siblings need to know about it in advance. I'm not dealing with them when push comes to shove, and we have to make hard decisions. I'm comfortable making hard decisions. I don't want to deal with the bullshit doing it."

This isn't the first time Maggie laid down the law with her family. She worked hard to set up the proper paperwork for her parents but reflects upon how she should have done the same for her and her husband before he passed:

"The irony in our situation was that we [Maggie and her husband] had just had an extensive family discussion with my parents on them having living wills and medical directives, making me the executor of both my mother and my stepfather. We had just had that conversation, and my husband had just turned 50, and we always had a joke that, you know, he was going to, you know, not live past 50. It was a running joke. And he actually dropped dead of a heart attack a month after he turned 50. And we had actually talked about that we need to do this for ourselves. So I traveled to really dangerous places for work. Because I was at the time 42, and he had just turned 50, and we're like, oh, we got a little bit of time. Um, but my parents didn't. So we really had to focus all of our energy on my parents. And they're both still alive and kicking, and here I am by myself."

Maggie and her husband were not weird in this case. Childfree individuals all too often put off things like wills, living wills, and the like. In cases such as Maggie's, this becomes even more important to address early when you are not legally married. Government and healthcare organizations often look for a next of kin and expect children. Maggie now had to deal with a lot of paperwork and hassle while she was grieving.

Maggie is amazing. She has been through a lot and was strong throughout. She encouraged me in my research to look at how it is different being a single Childfree woman. Maggie has an idea to buy a castle or some land as a great place for single women to live. I'd love to see that. Maggie has found a way to balance being childfree with work, and some of that may be a reflection of an understanding boss. She recalls a story about her first day on a new job:

"My boss came by on my first day. He recruited me to come and work for him. He had two or three kids at home. He had previously done a stint at the national security council in the White House when his kids were pretty little, so, you know, and he sacrificed time with his kids at that. So, we were talking, and he knew who I was as a colleague, but I didn't know if he knew anything about my home life. And somehow it came up that, you know, I said something like,

'Oh, it's just, just my spouse and my dog.' And he's like, Nope, it's not *just,* and I was like, well, what do you mean? And he goes: 'I don't care what you go home to. It can be a dog. It could be a cat. It can be a plant. It can be the newspaper, that's your business. And you go home at five o'clock or whatever that time is. But the flip side is, if you answer emails after that time, then that tells me you're on. Then you're responsible.' And so, his whole thing was, I don't care what you go home to. It's not my job to judge what you go home to. So, I tell that to every single person that reports to me, not my business what you go home to, it's your business on managing your work-life balance."

In the end, being Childfree works for Maggie:

"I love having a life where I have discretionary income, and I can kind of go do what I want. The only thing I gotta plan for is, like, my parents and my dog. And, you know, that's kind of, you know where I'm at. I have a pretty cool job. I travel to places most people can't find on a map, nor do they want to find on a map."

20

MARIA – A PORTRAIT OF GETTING STARTED

Maria

25, Single, Female, Texas

Associate's Degree

Translator

M aria is 25, loves cooking, travel, and making YouTube videos, and is originally from Japan, but grew up in Florida. She works as a translator and interpreter for healthcare and schools. So why did she decide to be Childfree?:

"One of the reasons is because you have more time for yourself and you can focus on the things you'd like to do and things you enjoy, especially with work. If you want to travel, you don't have to worry about childcare. And you don't have to worry about making enough money to support yourself and your child. I just think that I want to focus on myself right now, and I just really don't see how I can, like, manage to take care of the child and myself and manage my time efficiently. Life just feels hard. Even after college, I sometimes find it hard to manage time, but I can't imagine what it would be like if I had a child. I had a dog before, but you know, having a child is completely different from having a pet."

Was there a moment when Maria decided she did not want to have kids?:

"It was maybe like two years ago, I was talking with a friend. She doesn't have any kids. We were talking about our future, and the topic came up. I guess we both were working with minimum wage jobs at the time, both in school and all. And it was just thinking about our future and what we want to prioritize. Do we want to prioritize our careers, or do we want to have a family? Even do we want to keep relationships as well? I mean, unless you find your soulmate, it is hard. So I guess that's when I realized I want to just focus on what is important, my work and my life."

What does Maria see as the biggest benefit of being Childfree?:

"Well, I wouldn't say less stress because you would always have stress either way. So, I would say just having the flexibility to do things on your own time and being able to help your friends when you are on short notice. You don't have obligations other than work and having to pay bills and all that."

Does she have any regrets about her choice?:

"At the moment? No. Maybe, like, in a couple of years, like when I'm, like, 30, I might like to revisit the question."

Maria's dream is to start her own business. What type?:

"I would say either a hotel or a nail salon, like a beauty salon. I'm interested in beauty, and hair and nails make all that stuff. I enjoy making people feel beautiful. Help make their hair nice and all that. Or I would make a hotel that's kind of like a cruise where you can do a bunch of stuff and go bowling. Like an all-inclusive hotel, or you can do anything you want that's travel-related or maybe something like that."

When I asked what she thinks she needs to be doing differently now, Maria shared:

"I guess one thing is to budget. I haven't been good at that the past year, but yeah, I guess I would say to budget and try to save more money. I need to try to spend less on things I don't need."

What does she need to spend less on?:

"I guess, like, one thing would be like playing games on your phone."

It may be surprising to some, but spending money on games is a common area that can be cut back on. Maria thinks she could save $200 per year, but it might be thousands for others.

So what is holding Maria back from achieving her dreams of opening her own nail salon?:

"I don't have the finance, the money to start one yet, I guess. But I know about marketing, starting my own business, and all that. So, I guess I will have to invest."

Maria says she is about one-third of the way towards what she needs and plans to save until she is about 30. She does not have any debt and does not want to take out a loan to start the business. This is a good plan. In general, you should try to start a business "at the speed of cash." That means launching and growing at the rate you can afford without borrowing.

Maria is working hard at getting started towards her goals. Is she happy?:

"I think it's all up to you to be happy or not. It's all up to your actions and how you take on different situations in your life. It depends on how you interact with people and what kind of people you surround yourself with. At the end of the day, it's all up to you. It's up to you who decides like, oh, if you're happy or not"

What advice does Maria have for others?:

"You don't need to have a child to know what true love is. Having a dog and giving your attention and love is also possible. Not everybody has motherly instincts, and children are very expensive, and you will have a better chance of saving your money if you don't have kids. If you don't have kids, you can focus more on your career goals and self-care since you will have more time and money to spend on yourself and save money along the way."

21

MICHELLE – A PORTRAIT OF GOOD VIBES

Michelle
26, Married, Female, Florida
Bachelor's Degree in Communications
Airbnb Host and Brand Ambassador

Michelle has been married for almost four years and is currently changing careers. She enjoys a lot of hobbies, with figure skating and reading topping the list. Right now, she isn't sure what she wants to do, but she knows it wasn't her last career. Fortunately, her husband makes enough to allow her to grow (much as in the Gardener and Rose approach) and find her passion. In the meantime, she rents out two rooms in her house on Airbnb and acts as a brand ambassador.

Why did Michelle decide to be Childfree?:

"When I was younger, I thought I don't really like children, and at most, I'd have one. I was not really thinking it was an option [not to have kids], especially because I am Hispanic. In our culture, that's not really talked about a lot. When I got to college and just being in higher education, I was like, I have options. I have choices. I just do not want to be pregnant. It sounds awful. And then with climate change and all that, it's like a big concern, especially for people that are in our generation. Why bring another child into this world when you can, like, foster or adopt. Also, from a financial standpoint, I won't be able to devote time or money to my hobbies. There are many, many reasons."

What about her husband?:

"We are the same age. We met in college basically like the first day. We started dating, and we both realized we had no interest in children, which worked out. So we are both equally on the same page of not having children."

Was being Childfree part of why they got together?:

"It definitely came together further along. We've been together almost nine years, but when you're in college it's not really something you think about, you're just like, oh, let's not get pregnant. It's like the only concern. And then once like, you know, we age and like actually started taking life seriously, like, oh, we're actually on the same page about this. It's really important that it's discussed before you get married, but it kind of just happened. And I think we both lucked out."

Michelle still checks in occasionally to make sure they are still on the same page. But, as she says:

"He's like, absolutely."

So what is the biggest benefit of being Childfree?:

"The freedom to basically dive into anything you want. If I want a career change, I don't have another mouth to feed that I have to worry about. If I want to travel the world, I don't have to think about, oh, what am I going to do? Like, you know, with the child in tow. So things of that nature."

Any regrets about being Childfree?:

"No. We always talked about the rare event that we wanted to have a child in our lives. We have no hesitation in fostering or adopting. There are so many children in the world. Having that as an option made the decision a lot easier. Most likely we're not, 'cause children, ehh, but if we're 40 and bored, maybe."

Does she have a set of goals for her life?:

"I guess my goal will be to experience more things. I know you can do that with travel, but to generally experience more and try things out of my comfort zone. So maybe I'll do rock climbing, maybe skydiving, we'll see about that. But, then, on the financial side, I would like to pay off my house as soon as I can so that I can live a more free lifestyle. And then just try to make sure I don't go into debt."

The only debt they have is their house. When do they plan on paying it off?:

"It's a 30-year loan, but I'm hoping to do it in half the time and in a realistic manner. I get that a lot of people work really, really hard for like a couple of years to tackle it. But, like, my philosophy is to live our life if we can and have some balance. So I definitely want to get rid of it like a responsible adult, but not like killing myself to do it. At the end of the day, it's like a fixed price for the next 30 years. Whereas the rental industry is like a hundred dollars, two hundred, three hundred every year, it goes up. So that's why I'm not as worried. I also rent out my house, like two rooms on Airbnb. So that helps."

So, did they have a plan to be debt-free for a reason, or did they just fall into it?:

"I fell into it. I started watching more, like, financial YouTube channels. A lot of them were also geared toward women, and it resonated a lot with me because it felt like they had the same philosophy. Like not just to hustle, hustle, hustle, but to find the balance in life. Like, yes, you could still get, like, a coffee or spend money on skincare with, you know, stuff like that. Like it made it [financial planning] more digestible. So, when I started getting into that, it's kind of changed my mindset and helped me reach the financial goals we had at the time."

Michelle made sure to call out The Financial Diet as both being a resource for her and being Childfree.

Michelle's husband is probably even more into being debt-free than she is:

"He was kinda hesitant about even just having a mortgage. We are first-generation college students and all that, so we had to learn a lot of this financial stuff ourselves. And so, it could be a little daunting at first. And then you're just like, no, this is how the system works here, and we have to, like, keep up."

It is not only first-generation college students that need to learn this financial stuff themselves. In the U.S., we do not always teach people how to manage their finances. Michelle continues:

"They want to keep us financially illiterate to keep us in this cycle of debt and working and all that. And I definitely think it's done on purpose. I know when I was in middle school, though, we had a budget class, and I was like, this is like the best class I've ever taken because I was 13 at the time. And it just started that mindset. And not many kids get access to this or are even thinking about it."

Michelle and her husband see themselves as very lucky that they did not have student loan debt:

"We both got full rides to the university, so we were very lucky. So, we got to keep it this way and not mess up the chances and the opportunity we were given."

Michelle and her husband do their finances together but split tasks:

"I don't like the stock market. I'm not going to lie. It's not my cup of tea. I prefer to, like, forget about it and not have to watch something constantly. In terms of a set plan, our retirement funds are usually separate. Like I have the way I'm doing it. He does like the stock market more, so he's doing that. But all our finances are pretty open. We use Mint.com, and it does everything automatically, and it's visible for both of us. So it's all there. All the information is there, but how we do it is different in a way. But as long as we're checking in, no one's hiding anything.

We have like six accounts together. So, it's like one for bills. One for the bills that we Venmo. Then I have a savings account and another joint checking account. And then we each have our allowance account. So, from our paychecks and stuff, we have a set amount that goes to fun money. And it's like, no questions as to what you get to do with your money. So, everything's together except for our fun money. I would say I'm the bigger financial person. My husband grew up with not a lot of money, so I feel like it could be very daunting. He does want me to control our finances, but I'm very transparent."

While her husband grew up without much money, Michelle saw both having money and not:

"We grew up with a lot of money, and then the housing market crashed, and it was like we had no money. So I grew up with both, and I think that shaped me. Seeing both sides of the coin and then managing my money so that I could just be like normal and not like teetering from one side to the other. So I have had to start from zero a couple of times, and it's not a big deal. But, when you grow up with money, and then something happens, that can also be very scary."

What are her retirement plans?:

"Well, with the state of the world, you never know if you're even gonna make it to that age. And I feel like that's a sentiment many people my age, especially younger people, have with everything going on. If we do, I have other childfree friends where, like, we'll just live together. We'll take care of each other. Just because you don't have children doesn't mean you don't foster a community. I have friends who have children who will probably be a part of their lives."

Does she plan on not working in retirement?:

"I think it just depends. Maybe I want to work at a bookshop when I'm 60 years old. I probably won't stop working or traveling. I'll just slow it down. But, like, people who would just wait to live their life until when they retire are wasting the best parts of your life. Live when you have the energy. If they wait until they retire, they have the time and the money, but they don't have the energy to do it. So it'll just be like a balance."

Michelle is doing a great job at balance now. However, when her career wasn't working out, her husband encouraged her to quit:

"He noticed that the job had been a lot more stressful, especially in the last month. So, I was like, this job is being toxic. I started gaining weight because I've had no time to do anything else. And he was like, yeah, like I could see that you're quitting. So we crunched the numbers. It looks like I just won't be able to eat out as much anymore or do stuff, but I won't have to give up figure skating. I want to think about this. So just having the numbers running, I got on his health insurance instead, and we were able to make it happen."

This approach is what I call the "Gardener and the Rose." In this case, Michelle is the Rose and taking an opportunity to grow and find herself. Her husband is providing the support (gardening), which works for them. Later, they might switch. I think it is a unique part of the Childfree community (and lifestyle), which Michelle agrees on:

> "I think that does happen a lot in Childfree communities. There have been times when I was the only one working. We were younger and had less expenses, but I was the only one working, and he had a part-time job. So I had like two jobs or something, and it was just like back and forth. One time he got laid off, and I was the only one working, but then he was able to relax for maybe two weeks. And then he found a job. So that Gardener and Rose analogy is very accurate."

In the end, Michelle and her husband are pleased with their life. I asked her how she would sum everything up, and she said:

> "Good vibes. Just vibes here. Just feel out what you should do next and stuff like what's to come and stuff. Just feel it out. Good vibes."

22

MIRENA – A PORTRAIT OF OPTIONS

Mirena
21, Female, Single, Idaho
Bachelor's Student in Business (Marketing)

Mirena grew up in rural Idaho and is currently finishing up a Bachelor's degree in business, focused on marketing. In addition, she works as an intern at her university, helping with social media. In her personal life, she practices witchcraft and loves to pick up random hobbies (and changes her hobbies regularly). She recently got sterilized (via bilateral salpingectomy) and is looking forward to all the options her Childfree life gives her. Mirena doesn't know what the future has in store for her, but she's excited:

"I'm a passionate person about pretty much anything that I get into. I enjoy working, and I want to work, and I look forward to working. Whatever I do, I hope to go into a lucrative career field. I don't know exactly what that is yet. I'm exploring sales as a possibility... Over the holidays, I saw family, and they all asked me, 'What are you going to do once you graduate?' I have never had a definite answer to that question."

While Mirena does not know what the future holds for her, the one thing she is sure about is being Childfree. She has known she has been Childfree since 15:

> "I have this distinct memory that I identified as a Childfree person for the first time at 15. I was in our U.S. history class with this teacher whom I hated. He was talking about manifestos, but everything was revolving around [a discussion of] 'all you girls when you go out and have children,' and I was like, Nope, I'm not putting up with this. I am not having kids. It's not going to happen. And he was like, 'well, you don't know what you want because you're 15.' And I was like, no, I know what I want. So, I think that was the first time, like in my life, where I had been outspoken about it."

Mirena has a wide variety of reasons why she decided to be Childfree:

> "I have a general aversion to pregnancy. It grosses me out, and I never want to ever go through that, which is why I got sterilized a couple of weeks ago. I also couldn't raise somebody else's kids. So I don't really have an affinity towards children. I don't hate them, but I also, like, would never want to raise them."

Mirena has no regrets about her choice to be Childfree and only sees benefits:

> "Biggest benefit, in general, is freedom. When I graduate, I plan to put everything I own in a suitcase and move to some big city. I don't know which one yet, but you couldn't do that with kids. So I can do kind of wild things like that in my life. What else is good about being Childfree? I enjoy my peace and quiet. It's nice. And I don't have responsibilities."

Mirena also sees being Childfree as being connected to being a feminist:

"I'm very much a feminist. Another awesome thing about being Childfree is that I'm not supporting the patriarchy—things like patriarchal imbalances, the wage gap, and all that kind of stuff. A lot of the burden [for raising children] falls on women and not on men as much... Some feminists have kids, but I do think I'm a better feminist because I don't have kids."

Mirena would probably move to Portland, Oregon, and start her own coven in a dream world. Her coven (a group of witches) would be focused on community service, possibly based around a soup kitchen. I would not be surprised if Mirena did one day start a coven. She is currently looking at a career in sales as it pays well and is fairly secure.

The one sure thing is that Mirena will move to a big city. She grew up in rural Idaho and is ready for a change. But, to Mirena, the location is more important than the job she is doing:

"I think the location does matter more. I would never go live in a super rural area again. I would never do it. You can't drag me back to a rural area."

Mirena is looking for both a better level of services (including internet, banking, healthcare, etc.) than are usually found in a rural area, but she is also looking for a different culture and group of people:

"In rural places, I think people are very closed-minded in general. You will find exceptions, but I want to maximize the number of open-minded people. There's no diversity like everybody's the same. They all follow the same life script. They all look the same. They all eat the same. There's no diversity, and I need to go see things and experience things that aren't everything I grew up with."

Mirena is at a crossroads in her life. She knows she wants to move to a big city, but beyond that, who knows?:

"There's just so much uncertain about my future. Like everything is in limbo. I tell people don't buy me anything of value right now for Christmas because I'm probably not going to own it in a year or two... How am I going to know if I got to the right place? If it fits my criteria that I don't have to own a car and have a job that I can enjoy, that is okay. I need a job that challenges me for sure. I need a job that's, like, going to, like, stimulate my brain."

Mirena has thought through her options. She works in her university's career center, and everyone has seemed to offer her options. After that, it is just a matter of picking the right choice:

"I thought about the Peace Corps. And I've known people who did it, and I'm sure some of the programs are good. Where I work, we have a Peace Corps/AmeriCorps person. AmeriCorps is like the Peace Corps, but specifically within the states. And they do a lot of, like, education initiatives. The people I worked with have also talked to me about doing that kind of thing. So, I thought about it for some time. And then I was like, yeah, but I'd rather chase money. They live off a really low stipend. So, you live in poverty for a couple of years, but I want to experience financial freedom."

I asked Mirena about what financial freedom means to her and what it would take:

"How much money do I have to make to experience financial free-dom? I tend to say over a six-figure salary, but I know that that's not true. You can subsist off less than that. A lot less than that. But like I think, having a six-figure salary is my goal."

Where did the need for money and financial freedom come from?:

"I didn't grow up, like, poor. My parents are middle-class, rural Idahoans. My dad's a fish farmer, and my mom's a librarian, so they're not making a killing. My mom had insurance, so we never went without medical care. I mean, my dad was a very cheap person. So sometimes he'd be like, do you have to go to a doctor for that? It's like, no, I should go to the doctor for this, Dad. I didn't grow up without. Where did this desire for money come from? That's a really good question. I think part of it is, I do see money as a security thing."

Mirena doesn't have a set plan besides graduating and moving to a big city. However, she knows she does not want to work in chemistry (which is where she started) and is looking at business because it has more options:

"I got involved in chemistry and worked for the department chair. He was like, 'You're going to have to go to school for eight years, and you don't have options in this, and you don't have options in that.' So I was like, oh shoot, I need more options for that. What if this doesn't work out, and this isn't what I want to do? That's why I like business. It has lots of options."

Mirena is clear that being Childfree is the way for her. It allows her to explore, and it does not matter that her family is not supportive of her choice:

"No one in my family fully approves of me being Childfree. The least pissed-off person is still pissed-off that I got sterilized. None of them are wholeheartedly accepting of that."

But, that's okay for Mirena as she will live her life, and who knows where it will take her?

23

MOLLY AND JAMES – A PORTRAIT OF LOVE

Molly
34, Female, Married, New Jersey
Bachelor's in Diplomacy
Appraiser

James
53, Male, Married, New Jersey
Technology

Molly and James were a pleasure to talk to about their Childfree life. From the start, it is evident that they love both each other and enjoy talking about being Childfree. Molly and James have an extensive network of Childfree friends (including half of their book club) and are proud of how their life allows them to be generous with friends, families, and neighbors. Although Molly calls her spouse "James the Great," I will just call him James here.

This isn't their first marriage. Both Molly and James were married before. Even though Molly had decided after her divorce that she was done with men and planned on getting a lake house and a dog, it would be their dogs that brought Molly and James together. James "won" his Westie back after his divorce, and Molly had just rescued a 10-year-old schnauzer before they met. I'll let Molly share their meet-cute story:

> "So five days after getting my dog, in walks this gorgeous mountain of a man into the dog park. James is quite tall, and I'm not. James has this little tiny white, fluffy dog with the pink harness and the pink collar. We both kind of like each other and just start chatting. I'm very chatty, and we went to the dog park accidentally on purpose at the same time, every day for three weeks before we went out on our first date. James invited me over to the house for a puppy play date.
>
> I called him on Thursday. I told him, I've had a shit day. I'm in a shit mood. I feel like shit. I have a shit attitude. Do you still want me to come over? And he goes, yeah, maybe it will cheer you up. I walked into parmesan risotto and osso buco from scratch and a dozen roses. That was Thursday. I left on Tuesday. I met his family that weekend. We've spent about 12 nights apart since then. That was over six years ago. We have not had a single fight since then because we have nothing to fight about."

I'll admit I was skeptical about them not fighting in the years since, but as Molly put it:

> "We have separate finances and no kids. So we have nothing to fight about."

James goes on to explain that being Childfree was something they bonded over:

> "One of the very first conversations we had was about the fact that neither one of us wanted to have kids. So we got that out of the way

really early on. No surprises. With my first wife, when we got married, she swore she didn't want to have kids. And then she changed her mind after we got married. So that was a serious issue in our marriage."

Molly knew she didn't want kids from a young age:

"I've known it since I was like 12, 13 that I didn't want to have kids. In the home ec class where you learn how to swaddle a baby. I was like, I don't need to learn this. I will never use this."

Yet having kids would be an area of concern in her first marriage also:

"My first husband, he wanted [children]. So I was willing to compromise and have one because he was Eastern European, the bloodline very important."

The marriage ended before Molly had to compromise and have a child.

Molly and James couldn't be happier with their Childfree life:

"James and I have had so much fun being a Childfree couple because we can do whatever we want."

James and Molly are like a lot of Childfree couples. They are "married" without the legal piece of paper. Three years ago, they had the big party (after three years of cohabitating), but neither wanted to get legally married again. As James shared:

"I didn't want to get married the first time. And I got, I got pushed into it. And I said never again because I got put through the wringer during the divorce. It could have cost me a lot more than it did, but it still cost me quite a bit. So yeah. There's that old joke: Why is divorce so expensive? Because it is worth it."

Molly explains it this way:

"After several years of dating, I said, you know what? I, I do want to have a wedding. I do want to get married. I want to be able to call you my husband. So we, again, never had a fight. So we sat down, and we talked about what does marriage mean for us? And what we realized is that what we wanted was not necessarily the legal protections of marriage, but instead, what we wanted was the celebration of our love and us as a couple. So we chose not to get married legally, but we had a full wedding."

They were smart about it. They knew what they wanted (and did not). At the same time, they did the work to cover each other. Molly and James updated their wills, healthcare directives, and other legal documents while maintaining separate finances (and separate attorneys). While the house is in James' name (he had owned it for a decade before meeting Molly), she pays for other things in the household. And they are now looking to buy a second house in southern New Jersey, closer to family (which will be in Molly's name). James explains:

"We consider ourselves to be married and on a practical, functional level, we are married. Just not legally."

Molly and James have found an outstanding balance that reflects the yin and yang of their relationship. As Molly said:

"I'm more of a literature, history, international cultures, and also like weird shit [person]. And James is more of the physics, mathematics, and philosophy [person]. So as a result, because we have an interest in each other's fields, our car rides are amazing."

When asked if they have any regrets from being Childfree, Molly shared:

"I would say very occasionally I might feel that little broodiness. But that's why my dog's wearing a sweater right now."

James laughed and added:

"I would say that not only do I have no regrets, but the older I get, the more solidly I'm convinced that I made the right decision."

Molly and James are in a good financial situation. While they may not be entirely at the stage of financial independence, they are close and looking at when and how they might want to retire. The problem is that they both enjoy what they do, and James has worked hard at work-life balance. If they retired, what next? James is working hard to teach Molly about balance:

"I want to retire early and get out of the rat race and get off the hamster wheel. But at the same time, I want to enjoy my life while I'm living it... I've been teaching Molly about work-life balance for the last six years. She has gotten better because I met her. She was working like 80 hours a week and working seven days a week and stuff like that. And now she's taking like, you know, weeks off at a time."

Finances and retirement may be a math problem for James and Molly. A 20-year gap in their ages means that James may retire well before Molly. Add that to the fact that James's family is long-lived (with many family members living to well over 100 years old), and it is a different picture of retirement, as James shares:

"Given my life expectancy, I need to have enough money to live that long in terms of retirement savings and everything like that. So I have to put a lot more thought into how much money I have invested and put aside because, you know, I'm not going to live to seventies or eighties. I'll probably live to 100 or 110."

Molly says that works for her:

"I think my life expectancy is more in the eighties, which makes me happy because, with our 20-year difference, that's the same time I would probably also retire."

I can't fault their reasoning. They don't have many (or any regrets) about their life, and as Molly shared:

"Both of us have the very similar mindset of you should do everything to the fullest. You never know when there's going to be a car accident, or I don't know, a plane falling out of the sky."

I asked Molly and James to describe what Childfree Wealth means to them. Molly shared:

"Well, part of it is money. Absolutely. I had the goal of having a net worth of a million dollars by the time I was 50, and I hit it at 34. I had no student loan debt. I got rid of them by the time I was 30. So, as a result, that's a lot less worry that I have to deal with. To me, that is a form of wealth. I have the time to do what I want.

If I want to take a special project and work extra hours, I can. If James and I want to have a date day on Christmas Eve, we can just do that. We don't have to worry. That's the greatest form of wealth because I'm not sitting here pregnant, worried that there's going to be a miscarriage. I'm not worried about how I am going to save for college. I'm not worried that my child has slammed the door in my face."

And James added:

"Or worried about how they are doing in school both academically and socially."

Molly continues:

"The biggest form of wealth is that I can do what I want when I want, I can eat whatever I want for dinner. You know, I, I don't have to worry constantly."

James looks at Childfree Wealth in much the same way:

"It's (Childfree Wealth) just the freedom and flexibility to live the life that we want to live. And part of that is financial freedom. But as we said, part of it is also just the lifestyle, freedom, the ability to have a garbage day or just to chill and not have to worry about anything other than our little doggies. And they're pretty well-behaved."

Being Childfree isn't just a benefit to Molly and James but also others around them. James put it this way:

"Us being Childfree translates into us being more generous with our friends and family. We spend a lot more money on our family and spoiling our nieces, nephews, and doing things for friends or, like we mentioned, the block party [that Molly throws every year] because we have that extra financial freedom. So, we can be a lot more generous and spread the wealth a lot. So, we're a lot more generous with our friends or family than most people."

Being Childfree fits both Molly and James. Molly sums it up best:

"We love our relationship, and kids would change that dynamic. We love each other enough that we still live a life fulfilled... All of this means that we get to spend the most time loving each other and not focusing on other people. And it means that we have a much stronger relationship than anyone else because we don't fight because we do take these steps and don't have children. We're not sleep-deprived. Or having an argument at three o'clock in the morning about whose turn it is to burp the baby. You know, we get to enjoy just the warmth of being with each other, you know. [*When I asked the question*] What would you do if you had 24 hours left? Well, I would just spend it with you [James]. It [being Childfree] gives us that freedom for love."

24

REBEKAH AND MATTHEW – A PORTRAIT OF RECENTERING

Rebekah
32, Female, Married, Ohio
Bachelor's in Web Development
IT Security

Matthew
32, Male, Married, Ohio
CNC Programmer

Rebekah and Matthew have been married for three years. Rebekah works in IT security for a bank, and Matthew is a CNC programmer. They recently bought a house and are now working towards being debt-free by 40. They are working on setting goals together and recentering to refocus on the things that are important and to achieve a balance. They are Childfree and trying to enrich the world rather than adding to the suffering out there. As Rebekah shares:

"I think more than anything, we enjoy watching the world around us and being a part of enriching it. But, at the same time, I've become aware over my short life of just how much suffering there is in the world. So, that's been driving a lot of our decisions with, you know, not adding to the population. We both have siblings, he has two sisters, and I have three sisters. So, we've got a lot of people hoping to have kids and having kids. And a lot of our peers are doing the same. So, we definitely feel like we get to experience the joys of watching children, but we don't feel the need to do that ourselves."

Being Childfree isn't something they just jumped to. Rebekah's decision to be Childfree came from a lifetime of experiences:

"I think it was a long time coming for me. I grew up in a conservative home. I was homeschooled through the ninth grade. I went to a public college, but you know, there were a lot of preconceived ideas. I think that it was unspoken. It wasn't like our parents told us, yes, you're going to have kids. It just was kind of an understanding that that's where your life was headed. Even at a young age, I didn't feel motivated in that way. I was not super maternal... As I got older, I became more socially aware. Right after the Sandy Hook shooting, I looked at what happened, and I just said, this is not a hospitable place for children. That kind of sealed it for me."

Matthew's choice to be Childfree was more related to his experiences helping to raise his sister's kids:

"I was taking care of my sister's kids because she was in a situation that she couldn't. So when she had them, they were essentially newborns, and she couldn't do it. And at the time I was living with my parents, I had a part-time job, and it was up to me to care for them. I love both my nephews. So when it was my time to stop looking after them, I was so relieved. I was so done with changing diapers and burping."

Both Rebekah and Matthew had decided to be Childfree before they met. When they came together, it just seemed to fit. While they agree on not having kids, Rebekah sees the biggest bonus of being Childfree as the time it allows you, while Matthew sees freedom as the biggest benefit:

> "The time gained to focus on not just things that you care about personally, but others and people outside of your immediate area because you get tunnel vision. When you have a family to take care of, that's your world... I know it's a general statement because time can be applied in many different ways, but I think about the time for careers and each other. Time to hopefully go out into the world and help people that need help. I think ultimately it is where we want to be."

Matthew had first volunteered freedom, but how is that different than time?:

> "I would say, well, freedom is part of the time. In general, I like being free to take a nap when I want to take a nap and just be a little self-ish. You grow up, and you're told what to do all the time. It's just nice not to have to do anything sometimes. And that is so hard to do with kids."

Do they regret their choice to be Childfree? Matt provides his perspective on regrets:

> "I think a lot of regrets, especially for men, are around. Oh, I have to keep my bloodline going. And I had to have my DNA in a smaller object and watch it grow and push my beliefs on it. And all this other stuff. That desire has never been any desire of mine. I'm the only son and youngest of my family. So like I have no desire to just be like, I got to keep this name going."

Rebekah has no regrets but does have fears:

"I don't have any regrets at this moment in my life. I do have fears, just in the sense that I think a lot. Working in a bank, especially working in the security department, we're very aware of all the elder abuse that comes from it. And honestly, it comes a lot of times from families, right? From people in their own safe space that are stealing from them or not advocating for them in the correct way as either being power of attorney or whatever. I do worry about not having a close family member that could be counted on if we can't make sound decisions or whatever the case may be in our old age. That's my biggest worry. It's not a reason to have kids by any means."

Rebekah's fear is common. In general, Childfree individuals need to have a living will and will. A living will state your preferences of what should be done while you are still alive, while a will talks about your estate after you pass. You need to appoint someone as a medical proxy and possibly a durable power of attorney (POA) and executor with those documents. The problem is that both the medical and financial systems break down if there is no next of kin to make decisions. Childfree people should consider appointing a professional trustee and fiduciary (whom you pay) to ensure their wishes are followed. Rebekah explains she hasn't started looking into ways to address her fears:

"I haven't done a lot of research, even though this is a fear that is slowly preying on me. I know it's a long time off, but it is never too early to research and just to understand your situation. If you want to pay somebody, you got to have the funds to pay somebody. That's the other piece of building our wealth so that we can be as independent as we can for as long as we can."

I ask a series of questions about what people would do if they were financially secure, had five to 10 years to live, or had only 24 hours to live. After those questions, I asked Rebekah and Matthew to reflect on what they should be doing differently now. Rebekah had a

list of things to do differently, while Matthew did not. Rebekah
shared:

> "Financially, I think we've put some goals ahead of ourselves that
> we're working to achieve, and we're knocking them out. We didn't
> jump on saving for retirement fast enough and aggressively enough.
> I know finances are only one piece of it. There is a whole balance of
> time is money, but time is your life as well. It's not all about financial
> security. It is all also just about time spent. You can die with a pile of
> money and have lost years of your life getting there. So, I do balance
> those two goals pretty heavily in my mind. I think today we've got to
> do better budgeting and the way we handle our money. I think we're
> working on that, but you know, we slip up."

Rebekah and Matthew just recently combined their finances.
When a couple combines their finances, it is often less about the
accounts or accounting and more about having joint goals, dreams,
and planning. It tends to be rocky at first, so Rebekah's reflections are
normal. Rebekah shared:

> "Our bank accounts have not been together for most of our relation-
> ship. It is odd, given that we were very much on the same page
> regarding how we handle our money and are very transparent with
> our money. But, for whatever reason or another, we just didn't put all
> of our stuff together until recently."

Matt added on:

> "It's probably a little bit of, like, I don't want you judging me. Like I
> buy these worthless three-inch pieces of colored plastics [gaming
> miniatures]. They're not expensive, but it's more the amount I buy. It
> made me look at our finances and realize these aren't just my
> finances now. They're yours as well, and I should look at that and
> our goals."

Rebekah closed with:

"[combining our accounts] has clarified our common goals for sure."

It is okay for couples to combine their finances (or not). From a financial planning standpoint, if a couple decides not to combine their finances, they have separate plans and are closer to roommates. This does not imply any judgment on their relationship, only on financial structure. A legally married couple can manage separate finances, but keep in mind that it is not that easy in the eyes of the government. Even if you file your taxes under the status of Married Filing Separately, in many debts and financial situations, both part- ners may be on the hook. The bonus of doing things together is precisely what Matthew and Rebekah shared. It brought them together on common goals. It does take time and effort to recenter together and work together on goals.

So, what are their goals together? Rebekah shared:

"They are very career-oriented and saving-oriented right now. Our home is our only debt right now, just our mortgage. And we want to be debt-free. So that's a big goal of ours."

They are on the right page. The vast majority of my research on Childfree Wealth says that if you want to achieve financial indepen- dence, you have to do two things: 1. Get out of debt (and stay out), and 2. Max out your retirement plans. I shared these two things with them, and here was Rebekah's response:

"That's excellent! Those are exactly what we are working on, but it's so hard. He didn't get a degree, while I earned a Bachelor's degree and had student loans. We both had car loans plus the mortgage. It was a lot, and we've made really good progress getting all but the house paid. Then at the end of the day, we can be maxing out retire- ment. Getting out of debt 100% and then staying out of debt is hard. You're going to need more cars eventually. We need to get that savings up so you can pop by with cash and do it smart. But we're still learning. We didn't grow up wanting. We grew up moderately well off. But we weren't given strong examples of how to handle money by our parents. My dad handled the money 100%. I had no idea of what was going on. But, there were always some feelings of anxiety about what we could afford. Then on your side [Matthew's], I think it was similar. We were kind of learning on the fly here and still are."

Their experience growing up with money is entirely normal. Growing up, the only thing I learned was how to balance a checkbook, which is completely useless now. They are learning together now, which is excellent. The hard part is shifting from individual finances to doing things together. As Rebekah explained, she bought her first house at the age of 25 on her own:

"When we got together, we were only together a year before I was ready to buy my first house. I was 25. I had the down payment, and I'm like, hey, I'm buying a house. Do you want to come live with me? And that's what we did. The house was just in my name because we weren't married at the time. But at the end of the day, I was always like, if this goes south, this is my house."

Rebekah and Matthew are like many Childfree couples. They could live on one income, but now they are doing things together and finding the right balance. Being Childfree means that we have more options and could cut back on work (or even cut out one income) and be fine. The challenge is to find a balance between work, goals, and life. Both Rebekah and Matthew expressed that they would like to spend more time with friends and family. So why doesn't Rebekah cut back a bit on work to get that balance?:

"I'm salaried, but putting in extra hours to work towards promotions or things of that nature aren't necessarily required. So it may be possible to get that time balance back to what we wanted."

Towards the end of the interview, I reflected that it sounds like they are working on finding a balance, getting the right goals, and recentering on what matters. So I asked if that made sense and Rebekah replied:

"Absolutely. I can't tell you how much we were driven to spend money on things like what everyone else is doing. Everybody's going out to this thing. Everyone's going out to that. We love our friends. We love doing things. We would go. We would just be like, well, goals are secondary. That'll come later. Then like you said, recentering is like, Hey, no, let's think about it. When we stopped for a little bit, we found that we had extra money. And then when we started seeing that debt fall, that was addictive. That was like, oh wow, look at it, go away. Especially the student loans. I just started hammering the student loans away. Then when we got this stimulus, checks went right on the debt. It was just like, we don't need anything. Let's go. We didn't miss a day at work through the pandemic. We hate saying no to people when our friends are going like, hey, we're just doing this thing. Not that they would hate us if we didn't go, we just don't like to be that person. Well, no, again, we're not being drug out. Before, we were overextending ourselves hugely. Then once the pandemic hit and we got to stay home, I was like, I never want to go back to where my time is the same as everyone else's. 2021 came around, and everyone's like, hey, everything's opening back up. We have to figure out a way to reduce the number of things we're doing. Not to be miserly with our time, but to recenter, and to refocus on the things that are important and find a balance and not overextend ourselves, but also not being selfish."

25

RYAN A – A PORTRAIT OF FREEDOM AND NO REGRETS

Ryan A

47, Male, Married, Utah

Bachelor's in Marketing

Fractional Chief Marketing Officer

Ryan has been married to his wife, Anna, for 17 years. He works as a fractional chief marketing officer and runs his own consulting business. He and his wife work from home with their dog, a cockapoo named Bailey, when they aren't traveling and working from some far-off spot. Ryan works no more than 25 hours a week (and never on Fridays) and has reached financial independence. He has the freedom to do what he wants, when he wants, and lives a life of no regrets.

Ryan never wanted children:

"I never wanted children. I grew up in a conservative Christian environment where everyone had children, and it always just seemed terrible to me, to be completely honest. Everyone would say children are a blessing, but then their lives were kind of hell and miserable and terrible. You could see that they were constantly stressed and anxious and all these costs and all these problems and the kids had problems. So I just have no passion for this."

Being Childfree cost Ryan some girlfriends and changed his dating life:

"I've certainly lost several girlfriends over it [being Childfree] in college. They wanted to get married. I said, yeah, I just don't want to have kids. That was a deal killer for them, which is great. I couldn't care less. And so, when I met my wife, I had said, I have a strong desire to remain Childfree, and she did as well."

Ryan and Anna were married for five or six years before she changed her mind and decided she wanted kids:

"We got married. We were married probably about five or six years, and she reversed her decision on that [being Childfree]. She decided she wanted kids. As luck would have it, either positive or negative, we had major fertility issues. In the end, we were unable to have natural children. I was kind of [relieved], and she was kind of depressed about it for a while. But she has come to terms with it now, and for us, adoption and all that was just not an option. So, we just decided to live our best life, Childfree."

Ryan's situation is not unusual. It is a common concern among Childfree individuals that their spouse might change their minds later in life. However, Ryan was very clear and that he was Childfree, but he was willing to have a child for Anna:

"It took me a little bit of time just to come around to the idea [of having a kid]. Eventually, my thinking was, either she can be miserable, or I can be miserable. And if she's miserable, we're both going to be miserable. I thought I could always just get an office outside the house. I love working from home, but I thought, there's an office building a mile away, so I can do that and still have a largely childfree existence. I had told her if we're doing this, we're having a kid, no plural, just one. She had agreed to that. I think ultimately that if we had had a kid, it would have been okay, but we didn't, and it's all good."

I asked Ryan if there was ever a moment during his debate with Anna over kids where he thought about splitting up:

"Absolutely not. My wife and I are soulmates. We are supposed to be together. I don't believe that there's just one person for everyone or even one person for anyone, but my wife and I are a good match. And ultimately, it came down to her happiness. And if I can do something that supports her happiness without making my life too terrible, I'm going to do it. And the reality is I can afford a nanny. I can afford childcare. We are in a financial situation where she could have stayed home if she wanted to. So we had some flexibility there."

While Ryan is still adamantly Childfree, he shared:

"I'll tell you at this stage in my life, there's a part of me that wishes the kid had worked out, the singular kid. I think that at this point in my life, it would be potentially more fulfilling, but there, there was no way to do it."

I asked him why he thinks it might be more fulfilling:

"I have no clue. It's kind of like all the years I lived in a condo with no yard and worked 80 hours a week. I always thought to myself, you know, it'd be nice and fulfilling to have a dog. I've always liked dogs. I grew up with a dog, and then when I finally got a house, I got a dog, and it was great. So I just have that same general feeling based on nothing."

Ryan has no interest in adopting and isn't rethinking being Childfree, but he sees his values shifting as he gets older:

"I feel my value system changing as I get older and shifting as I get older. As I get older, I would say I become more socially liberal. As I get older, I become more focused on friends and family and much less focused on making money and accumulating things. In fact, I'm trying to get rid of things. So, I think that it's part of that, that spiritual shift, maybe it is wisdom, maybe it is experience, maybe it is something else, I don't know."

Even with all that in mind, Ryan does not have any regrets. He does not see a value in having regrets in life:

"I'm not a regret type of person. I think that hindsight is much better than foresight, but I don't tend to live with much regret in general. I've always tried to make the best decision I could with the information I had at the time. In doing that, you know that you're not going to get it right every time. So I think that in, in doing anything, you know, the fact that I became a marketer, not a doctor or I became a marketer, not a lawyer, I became a marketer instead of something else, you know, that you always take something off the table and you leave everything else. I realized that's just how it is. So in making this choice, I don't have a lot of regret because I'm just not a regret personality. People say, oh, don't you wish you would've bought Netflix stock when it IPO'd? And I'm like, of course, I do. But I'm a Vanguard investor. So I didn't, and I'm fine with my choices there. No regrets."

Instead of regrets, Ryan sees the benefits of being Childfree as freedom and flexibility. He and his wife have the freedom to do whatever they want, including traveling and working from anywhere:

"A few months ago, I'm thinking, eh, it's getting cold. Let me book a month in Palm Springs. So I just popped on my app on my phone, found a place, booked it. I said to the wife, let's go, and we left. I can put my entire office in a backpack, and we're out of here. We go and sit in Palm Springs for a month and do whatever. I can do anything like that."

Ryan is living a life I call FILE rather than FIRE. FILE is Financial Independence, Live Early, versus Retire Early. If FIRE is an on/off switch for work, FILE is a dimmer switch. He did "retire" before but needed the stimulation of work on his terms. He enjoys being a marketer:

"I could bang off and not work anymore, and I'd be fine. You know, we may not have as many, our trips might be a little more scaled back and some of our other things, but I'd be fine if I didn't work anymore. But it's nice to be able to choose what I want to do and whom I want to do it for. And to be able to do it for 20 or 25 hours a week. I have a few collaborators in my business, and I've taught them that 25 hours is my outside maximum. If there's an emergency, if a client needs something, if something is burning down, if I've worked my 25 hours, I'm done. I don't work Fridays, And I don't work before 10:00 AM ever for any reason. Those are my boundaries. It's a pretty nice thing to be able to do in your forties and to have that flexibility."

I pushed Ryan on his boundaries a bit, and he did not budge. He has a well-defined set of values, and sticks by his limits, even if it costs him business:

"I've done this for 15 years now. In my first couple of years in business, I had some client management challenges and quickly learned that you have to have hard and fast rules that are inflexible. As soon as we put those into place, honestly, I've never really had much of a problem ever since. A few years ago, I had one client on the East Coast that wanted to meet early in the morning. Eventually, we had to part ways."

Ryan can do this because he is financially independent. Part of that may be due to not having kids, but a more significant part is that he followed a simple financial plan all of his life. He stayed out of debt and invested in the stock market (Vanguard funds primarily), real estate, and businesses:

> "I'm still following the same plan that I created in college. I created my financial plan literally when I was 21 or 22 after somebody gave me a copy of [the book] *The Millionaire Next Door.* I read that, and I was like, wow, this is kind of cool. And then learned about John Bogel, Vanguard, and all of that. I thought, well, this is, this is pretty cool too. I bought into a real estate project with my mom when I was 19. I had a job, and you know, just kind of have continued along that same path. I know what works for me. It's multi-family property, Vanguard funds, business ownership, DONE."

Ryan was also debt-free from his mid-twenties and never had a mortgage. He started in a "small, cheap condo" and now lives in a $1.2 million house that he and his wife gutted and then remodeled with a completely custom interior. He shared that after posting in some FIRE groups online, he got quite the reaction for not believing in debt:

> "They're angry that I don't believe in debt. And I don't believe in business debt either. I've had people that are very, very angry. They're like, well, how can you not have debt? It's like not having skin or something [to them]. Debt has been so culturally ingrained. My first job out of college, the worst job of my life, was working in the pharmaceutical industry, peddling drugs for Johnson and Johnson. When I was in that job, I wound up thinking to myself, you know what? These drug companies were trying to own everything. They want to own the medical schools. They want to own the doctors. They want to get to the point where all the doctors know how to do is prescribe pills. They don't know anything about holistic wellness. They don't know anything about functional medicine. It should be pills, pills, pills. And I feel like our debt system and our

financial system has done the same thing to our people. It's so ingrained that, you know, you should be able to have it now, right now, there's no waiting. There's no saving. You're entitled to having it now and paying all these minimum payments, debts, and interest. There is this belief that there is good debt. A student loan is good debt, an auto loan is good debt, and a mortgage is good debt. I'm like, nah, I don't buy any of that."

Ryan has been faithful to his word and has never paid a penny of mortgage interest in his life. He still drives the Lexus ES that he and his wife bought 20 years ago for $17,000 in cash. It isn't that he does not have the money. He just doesn't see the value in a new car:

"I've got a $1.2 million house that is paid for. I have a million-dollar rental property that is paid for. I've got seven figures of business equity. I've got another seven figures in my stock portfolio. My net worth is probably in the $5 million range, but I don't see the value in spending money on a car. A car that I don't need, and we hardly ever drive."

Ryan still enjoys himself. He and his wife travel extensively, he loves collecting watches, and they do what they want. Living that FILE life works for him. Ryan is living a life of freedom, with no regrets.

26

RYAN G – A PORTRAIT OF SUCCESSFUL LAZINESS

Ryan G
43, Male, Married, Oklahoma
Bachelor's in Management Information Systems
Software Implementation

Ryan's portrait requires a bit of a disclaimer to start. I call this a portrait of successful laziness. Laziness, in this case, is not a derogatory comment but a reflection of a way of life that Ryan described to me. Ryan's life might fit "work smarter, not harder" but with a twist. He has found ways to "check off" many of the common steps in life and work, not to do more, but just to enjoy his life. I found myself envious at times of the balance he has achieved.

Bill Gates is often credited (although with some debate) for the quote, "I choose a lazy person to do a hard job. Because a lazy person will find an easy way to do it." Ryan explains it this way:

"Let's say you have to water your lawn every day. You could water your lawn, and you care about your plants. You don't want them to die. So, you're willing to put in the effort. Even though you're lazy, you could water your lawn every day. Or you could put in a lot of work right now to put in a sprinkler system. The system is more work upfront, but it's less work overall. And that's kind of the mindset you have to be to be a successful, lazy person. It is not, what's less effort [now], but what is less effort over a lifetime."

Ryan is Childfree but did not decide not to have kids. As he puts it:

"It's not like I ever thought about having children and decided against it one day. I've always never wanted children."

Ryan has been married for six years, and being Childfree was part of how they met:

"I found her using online dating. One of the search criteria was, 'does not want kids.' So, she's not wanted kids, as long as I've known her. But, it never occurred to me to ask if that's how she's always felt, or if she changed her mind at some point."

It also wasn't about the benefits of being Childfree:

"I didn't do a cost-benefit analysis to say, well, I kind of want kids, but I'm willing to give up the time and money. It was, I don't want kids, end of the story. And there are benefits to it, but I didn't do it for the benefits."

That isn't to say that Ryan and his wife did not benefit from being Childfree. They are in an excellent financial situation due to their choices and a bit of sound investing. Ryan and his wife both work with software implementation, but their finances allow them additional options. Ryan shared:

"She [Ryan's wife] is taking a break from work, and we're unsure, she's going to go back or not. We reviewed our finances. She was already struggling with work, with the pandemic, stress, politics, and everything. She needed a break, and we reviewed our finances. And if we're frugal, we could probably retire. So it may be that she permanently stopped working, and I may stop within the next year or three."

When they met, they each had their own home, but once their primary residence is paid off, retirement becomes a real option (in their early 40s):

"We each own a home, and we're thinking of selling hers and using the money to pay down this house. And then we'll be close to paying it off. I may work 'til it's paid off, or I may pull money out of savings. Once our house is paid off, really healthcare is our only real serious expense."

Healthcare expenses have become a recurring theme in many of my interviews. It seems like a combination of the cost and the unknowns impact early retirement decisions. Ryan puts it this way:

"I mean, if we had universal healthcare, retirement would be absolutely for sure. Without it, it's one of those things... Well, we think we can swing it, but it'll be a little bit tight, and it's going to be our biggest line item by far."

Ryan is very close to financial independence and retirement. I wouldn't be surprised if he has already accomplished it by the time this book is published. So, what would retirement look like for him?:

"Our life would essentially be the weekend seven days a week. For me, that means waking up in the morning, doing some housework, watching TV, playing video games, and inviting my friends over. If they're free, you know, or read books. That kind of would be my life, but seven days a week and work on my hobbies. I used to paint miniatures. I kind of stopped, but I might get back. If I had more money, I would do more. But the goal is to live our current middle-class lifestyle without working. And my middle-class lifestyle is after my responsibilities are done. It's board games, video games, and D&D [Dungeons and Dragons], and the big downside would be it wouldn't be the weekend seven days a week while my friends work. If they could retire too, it would be like Monday is D&D, Tuesday is Pathfinder, and Wednesday is this other game. Thursday is a rest day, and Friday, you know...."

Ryan has always known he wanted to be retired:

"I've wanted to retire since I was a teenager since before I had my first job, I knew I hated working since before I even tried it... So, I learned about IRAs and opened a Roth, and started contributing the max contribution from that point forward. Once I got my current job, which I've had for about 18 years, they gave me a 401(k). So, I started with the minimum to get matching and then increased it and was like, you know, I could probably contribute more. So, by my late twenties, I was contributing the max and then just been investing. I've had some luck with my investments. So, I've managed to accumulate a fair amount. I didn't even know about FIRE or that FIRE was an acronym 'til a few years ago."

Ryan may be doing the concept of FIRE, but the process and Subreddit communities just don't fit him:

"Honestly, a lot of those people are real overboard. Like, yeah, I'm going to retire because I'm going to cut every expense, and I'm going to make my own soap, and I'm going to work hard. My goal is to minimize how much effort I have to do. And honestly, a lot of the things they do seem like more work than a job."

Ryan has made an art of balance and not working too hard while moving towards retirement:

"I mean, I'm kind of lazy. So I'm taking the easiest path to retirement. Frankly, it was just getting a desk job and then taking as much money as I could and investing it. And I am not putting hard work into it. And it's worked out, right? My investments are worth a fair amount at this point. My desk job is fairly low effort, but it can get stressful sometimes. It's hard work, but it's still not as hard of work as some people who do physical work that I'm unwilling to."

Laziness isn't a negative in this case. Instead, it is a way of life that has a balance:

"I mean, it [being lazy] is a bad thing, but it has not held me back much. I'm lazy but responsible. So it hasn't stopped me from doing the necessary things to be successful. Maybe a good life. I mean, if you're lazy and a freeloader, that's obviously bad. Or if you're so lazy, you don't accomplish your goals. But I, I did accomplish my goals. I mean, I'm lazy, but I still graduated from college, got a house, and still have a decent job, which I'm holding down. It's just kind of how I want to live in a sort of a lackadaisical life of indulgence."

Ryan wouldn't change much. The only thing he might change in his life is to exercise:

"Exercise. I know I should, but I hate it so much. But one of my fears is that I'm going to be wealthy and then die. Right. And be like, yes, finally I'm rich, then a heart attack, you know? Or, or even if I don't die of a heart attack, that I will be one of those old people who sit in their chair and drools. 'Cause it takes too much energy to get up, and they don't go upstairs."

I asked Ryan to define Childfree wealth. His answer fits his approach:

"I don't really associate those two things together, even though they're obviously linked. I was not childfree with wealth as a goal. And when I plan for wealth, I didn't think about [being Childfree]. It was more like; I don't want to work, and I don't want kids, and those not having kids have it real easy. So I just decided not to have kids. And I mean, that just happens, right? You don't even have to do anything to not have kids. And then focusing on retirement, I, you know, did what I said. I try to find a job with the highest pay-to-effort ratio. And I put a lot of that money in the stock market. And I didn't really plan for being childfree, so I'll have more wealth, or I should [be Childfree] in order to get more wealth."

While retirement was something Ryan wanted all his life, it isn't that he is a super goal-driven person:

"I'm not driven. I'm not someone who feels much sense of accomplishment. Usually, when I do something, I feel relief that it's over. People are like, yeah, I succeeded at X. Isn't that amazing? And I'm usually like, oh god, finally done. Right. So the lack of a sense of accomplishment means that I don't set out to accomplish things. But that's not strictly true. I mean, I play video games, and I want to win. And I'm like, yeah, I beat the final boss, and I get something out of it. But it's, it's much more muted, I think, than some people I'm not like, yeah, I finally achieved this thing. Woohoo. It's more like, yay. I finally checked it off my list. So after [retirement], my goal would be maintenance. Keep the house clean and maintained, keep my marriage happy, keep the cats fed."

Ryan didn't follow a financial plan or even have a budget. He knows he needs to look at budgeting if he is going to retire, but so far, his focus has just been on maxing out his retirement and living his life. He's got Excel spreadsheets to track everything (he likes spreadsheets) and had a friend who is a CFP® professional weigh in on his path and provide some tweaks. Ryan doesn't have a long-term care plan (beyond his investments) and figures they can address that as they get older.

I have to admit that I had a bit of trouble reflecting on my interview with Ryan. I am also a "work harder, not smarter" person (I credit Scrooge McDuck with introducing me to that), but it is so I can achieve more to then relax and enjoy. I've always been goal-driven. I went through a bit of a mid-life crisis after achieving my goals. I have now shifted towards helping others to achieve their goals. In my mind, reaching your financial goals requires a plan, budgeting, and constant learning.

Ryan decided as a teen that he wanted to retire. It wasn't even indeed a goal, just a box to check off. He has gotten there (or almost) and now is looking forward to a life of gaming and friends. He may not have followed the "standard" path, but he did great. Next time I'm in Oklahoma, I'll have to look him up for some gaming, but I will probably need to learn to chill first.

27

APPENDIX A – RESEARCH PLAN AND INTERVIEW QUESTIONS

R esearch methods

THE PURPOSE of this phenological study will be to understand the lived experiences of Childfree individuals, couples, and groups related to setting and achieving personal, professional, and financial goals. In particular, the study aims to define "Childfree Wealth" as a reflection of these goals (and how to achieve them).

RESEARCH QUESTIONS INCLUDED:

- What is it like to be Childfree?
- What is truly important to Childfree individuals, couples, and groups (what is "Childfree Wealth")?
- How does being Childfree impact the achievement of goals (personal, professional, and financial)?

- What support is needed by Childfree individuals, couples, and groups to achieve their goals?

Sample

The sample will consist of Childfree Individuals, Couples, and Groups living in the United States aged 18 and older. For the study, Childfree is defined as "not having children (biological, adopted or step) and not planning on ever having children." Convenience and snowball sampling will be utilized until saturation is achieved.

Data Collection and Analysis

Data collection will be completed using an online survey and a semi-structured interview. The survey will provide both quantitative descriptive data and qualitative short answers. After completion of the survey, participants will be able to volunteer for a 45-60 minute interview. A constant comparative method will be utilized to inform and improve interview questions throughout.

Survey data will be collected through Jotform and anonymized. Interviews will be completed via Zoom, recorded, and transcribed for analysis. Participants will be able to choose their own pseudonyms to maintain anonymity throughout.

Data from participants will be triangulated by observations of the community online, literature review, and checking for continuity between survey and interview data.

Data from the surveys and interviews will then be coded. Coded data will then be analyzed to look for themes and patterns. Finally, themes, patterns, and quotes from both the surveys and interviews will be utilized to illustrate the findings and answer the research questions.

Outcomes

The goal of the study is to provide an in-depth analysis of the lived experiences of Childfree individuals, couples, and groups. The data will be presented in book format, structured for readability and applicability of a wide population.

SUBJECTIVITY STATEMENT

My wife and I are Childfree. Being Childfree ourselves brings a series of biases that need to be controlled for. My own personal experiences shaped some of the interview's initial questions. A constant comparative approach will be utilized to help improve the interview tool over time and control for biases.

Additionally, I am a qualitative researcher, an adult learning practitioner, and CERTIFIED FINANCIAL PLANNER™. As a researcher, my goal is to look at the sample objectively, but I will actively comment out my own thoughts and biases as data is analyzed. As an adult learning practitioner and CERTIFIED FINANCIAL PLANNER™, I will have to make an active effort to prevent trying to "teach" or "inform" participants as they are interviewed. The goal is to hear from the participants, not to share information.

SEMI-STRUCTURED INTERVIEW QUESTIONS

Introduction: Thank you for being willing to do this interview. I truly appreciate it.

The information you provide will be used to create a book about Childfree Wealth and Finances. Additionally, it may be used in blogs and derivative works. This interview is being recorded and will be transcribed later. Some of the questions may be similar to the survey, but the intent is to go deeper into a discussion.

When you booked, you chose a pseudonym of <> I will use that throughout. Do you have any questions for me?

Q1. Tell me about yourself (i.e., how you would introduce yourself at a social gathering).

Q2. Why did you decide to be Childfree?

Q3. What is the biggest benefit of being Childfree?

Q4. Do you have any regrets about your choice?

Q5. We are going to shift a little and talk about your life goals and life planning. There are three questions created by George Kinder that I'm going to read, and I encourage you to take time and think through your answers:

1. Imagine you are financially secure, that you have enough money to take care of your needs, now and in the future. How would you live your life? Would you change anything? Let yourself go. Don't hold back on your dreams. Describe a life that is complete and richly yours.

2. Now imagine that you visit your doctor, who tells you that you have only five to 10 years to live. You won't ever feel sick, but you will have no notice of the moment of your death. What will you do in the time you have remaining? Will you change your life, and how will you do it? (Note that this question does not assume unlimited funds.)

3. Finally, imagine that your doctor shocks you with the news that you only have 24 hours to live. Notice what feelings arise as you confront your very real mortality. Ask yourself: What did you miss? Who did you not get to be? What did you not get to do?

Q5b. Is there anything you think you need to be doing differently in light of those questions?

Q6. I am trying to define what Childfree Wealth means to people. It may have a financial component, but for most people, a good, wealthy life means more. What does Childfree Wealth mean to you?

Q7. Do you have a set of goals for your life? What are they? What is stopping you from achieving them?

Q8. Do you have a comprehensive financial plan you are following? Can you describe it? Why/Why not?

Q9. What are your retirement plans?

Q10. What are your long-term care plans (who is going to take care of you when you are older)?

Q11. Who is counting on you to take care of them? (What are you going to do for elder care for your parents/family?)

Q12: What question should I have asked that I did not?

Q13: Is there anything else you would like to share?

Thank you for completing the interview. I hope it wasn't too difficult. I am looking for more people to fill out the survey and interview. If you have any other childfree friends that might be willing to help, I would appreciate you sharing it with them.

28

APPENDIX B: FILE VS. FIRE

I t used to be that the goal was to retire and "get the watch." People would work 25 years at one company, pay their bills, and retire (often with a pension). Those days are gone. Retirement is no longer guaranteed for anyone and may not even be an option for many. Even for those who may be able to retire, it may not be the right choice.

The FIRE movement (Financial Independence, Retire Early) has grown in popularity lately. The concept is simple: Grind, hustle, and save now so that you can retire early. Sacrifice now for retirement early. The principles of FIRE are sound. There are even variations, including Lean FIRE, Barista FIRE, Chubby FIRE, Fat FIRE, and others. Effectively, each level of FIRE reflects a different life in retirement, with Lean being closer to living off ramen noodles and Fat FIRE having one's own private chef. The bottom line for FIRE is that the goal is to retire early and "turn off" work, like a light switch.

Retirement is not the goal for everyone. As I found in my research on Childfree individuals, many people seem interested in following their passions. Following their passions might be a career they love or running their own business. The difference is that they are okay with working and would be happy to keep working as long as possible. I had a great conversation with Ryan A, who explained that he could retire but he loves what he does. His answer was to pick the clients he works with, work no more than 25 hours a week, and never work before 10:00 am or on Fridays. He is fine if clients stop using his services (they have) and he works remotely from wherever is nice at the time (most recently Palm Springs, CA).

FILE (Financial Independence, Live Early) is a better option for those who don't want to retire. FILE prioritizes financial independence to live a life you enjoy, now and in the future. It may mean making the same sacrifices as a FIRE life, but with a different goal. If FIRE is an on/off switch for work, FILE is a dimmer switch. It is about finding a balance between time, freedom, and money.

The commonality between FIRE and FILE is the FI: Financial Independence. Financial independence means that you have managed your money to a point where you can make ends meet and don't have to worry about finances every day. That may seem like a luxury to many, but it is possible with careful budgeting, staying out of debt, and saving/investing. Financial independence happens when you are intentional and follow a plan. It isn't exactly sexy, but spending less than you make and saving for the future is the bottom line. Your behaviors with money will determine whether you achieve financial independence.

FILE is different because you can enjoy your life before you retire (if you ever do). Your goal in FILE is not stopping work at some arbitrary age (or net worth), but is instead living your best life both now and in the future. That changes the way you save and invest. Instead of investing everything in a retirement plan, you might invest in yourself or your business idea. This investment in yourself will slow down your progress towards retirement but may lead to a more fulfilling life now. It does require that you have faith in yourself and that you can achieve FILE, which may be the hardest part.

SOME QUESTIONS TO ASK YOURSELF:

- Do you want to retire? If so, when? And what do you want it to look like?
- What do you want to do if you don't want to retire? What is holding you back?
- Would you prefer to have more money or follow your passions?
- What are you willing to give up now for your ideal future life?
- Are you happy?

The problem for many people is that they cannot see a different future. Retirement looks attractive as at least it is an endpoint. But if you are not happy now, why wait to change it? The challenge with FILE is that you have a chance to do what you want when you want if you are willing to change. You can keep chasing more zeros in your bank account, but will it truly make you happier? It may seem crazy to take a pay cut, but if you would be happier doing something else (which pays less), why not do it? You might not be able to afford as much "nice stuff," but what is your happiness worth?

SOME TIPS TO ACHIEVE **FILE:**

- Set a budget and live within it. It does not have to be overly restrictive, but you need to know your Musts, Shoulds, Coulds, and Won'ts.
- Get out of debt. Debt is stealing from your future. If you want to achieve financial independence and do what you love, you need a solid foundation that does not include debt.
- Make a plan. Have a financial plan that reflects your ideal life. Set guardrails for what you can (or can't) spend. Set goals and measure your progress towards them.
- Save and invest. Investing in FILE may be just as much in you and your ideas as it is in the market. Saving for the

future (rather than retirement) may also require different investments and combinations of taxable and tax-advantaged accounts than the "norm."

- Celebrate your wins. Celebrate when you achieve milestones and remind yourself why you decided to follow a FILE life.
- Live your own life. Comparison is the thief of joy. Live your own life by your standards and your plan. The only person you need to impress is yourself.

29

APPENDIX C: THE GARDENER AND THE ROSE

Being part of a Childfree couple allows you to have different options in life. You get to choose how you want to live your life. The only thing you truly must worry about is yourself and your partner. The problem is that it can be difficult for both you and your partner to achieve your dreams, especially at the same time. To find a balance, my wife and I have adopted a Gardener and Rose approach.

The approach isn't new and was initially called the gardener and the flower. My wife isn't just any flower, so we call it the Gardener and the Rose. The basics are simple. For a Rose to bloom, it needs a Gardener to tend to it. The Gardener creates a safe environment for the Rose to grow and bloom within. The needs of the Rose may change over time, and the Gardener needs to be able to adapt.

For my wife and I, we are both PhDs. It is nearly impossible to find two careers, at the same location, at the same time, that allows two PhDs to use their degrees fully. For most, this results in a "trailing spouse" in a dual-career couple. In academia, one spouse gets a job, and the other hopes for a "spousal hire." Spousal hires are rare, and the trailing spouse has to make sacrifices to make it work. The result is that someone gets their dream job, and someone gets a job.

We have adopted the Gardener and Rose approach with the understanding that we will take turns in both roles. So one of us gets to grow and bloom, while the other provides support. Most recently, my wife was offered her dream job 1,200 miles away. Since it was an excellent chance for her to grow and bloom, we packed up our dogs (you need to see two Mastiffs in the back of a Prius) and our cat, and moved. Luckily, I can work from anywhere as I run my own company, and most financial planning is done via Zoom now.

Being the Rose does not have to be about jobs or making more money. It can be about growing in any way you want. My wife knows that in 15 years, I'm taking my turn as the Rose. That means that at 59 and a half, I'm truly retiring and doing the Great Loop. The Great Loop is about 6,000 miles of boating down that goes around half of the U.S. It means living on a boat for a year or more. It is most certainly not a good financial move, but it is what I want to do.

There is some fairness in this "rotation" of Gardener and Rose. We each get our chance to grow. Each couple has their own list of Gardener roles, but it may include things like maintaining the house, running errands, cooking, and more. In theory, if you make enough money, you may be able to hire out some (or all) of the Gardener roles, but that is much later in life.

It is also not about traditional gender roles. I will admit that many people were surprised that I would move for my wife's job. I don't get it, but there are still those who have set pictures of gender roles. I figure that if we already picked not to follow the LifeScript™ by being Childfree, we can choose whatever roles make sense without following the script.

What does this mean for you? If you are a DINK (Dual Income, No Kids) couple, it may be worth having a conversation about the Gardener and the Rose. Which one of you is doing which role now? Do either of you have bigger dreams or wants? Do both of you get joy from your jobs, or do you need a change? What about going back to school? Or starting that dream small business? Or...

In most couples, I find that either spouse is willing to sacrifice for the other, but not for themselves. If John's wife Jane wants to follow her dreams and be the Rose, then he is 100% behind her. If, on the other hand, John wants to be the Rose, then Jane is 100% behind him. The hard part is who goes first and admits they want to be the Rose.

Chances are you know which one of you is feeling restless and needs the change. Lay out the Gardening task and Rose opportunities. Set a plan for both. If possible, include a timeline. Commit to taking turns. The Rose can still do some dishes, but you need to figure out what support they need and what they need to stop doing.

Taking turns allows whoever is in the Rose role to focus on themselves and on growing. It relieves a bit of the pressure and feelings of being selfish. You know that both people get their chance to be the Rose in their own way. Be careful if someone only wants to be the Gardener (or Rose). We can all be a bit selfish in this process, and fairness should be considered.

Is it possible to have a balance? I don't know. I find that achieving a true balance within a couple (where they each do half Gardener/half Rose) means a series of sacrifices and compromises that are not always even. I hear things like, "I'm okay with my choice..." Okay is fine, but I'm not sure okay reflects true joy. I'll also hear things like, "well financially, we can't...." I then do the numbers, and there usually is an option if they are willing to make sacrifices together.

The challenge is not to settle for okay. Instead, choose joy in your life. Take turns and be your best self, whatever that is.

ABOUT THE AUTHOR

Jay Zigmont, Ph.D., CFP®

Dr. Jay, and his wife are Childfree and live in Water Valley, MS with their two mastiffs. He has a Ph.D. in Adult Learning from the University of Connecticut. He is an Advice-Only, Fee-Ony, Fiduciary, CERTIFIED FINANCIAL PLANNER™ and Childfree Wealth Specialist. He founded Live, Learn, Plan, and Childfree Wealth, a life and financial planning firm specializing in helping Childfree Individuals.

He has been featured in Fortune, Forbes, Business Insider, Wall Street Journal, CNBC, Woman's World, Investors Business Daily, FinancialPlanning, and many other publications.

Visit Childfree Wealth at
https://childfreewealth.com.

Disclaimer

Live, Learn, Plan, LLC ("Live, Learn, Plan") is a registered investment advisor offering advisory services in the State(s) of Mississippi and in other jurisdictions where exempted. Registration does not imply a certain level of skill or training. The presence of this book on the Internet shall not be directly or indirectly interpreted as a solicitation of investment advisory services to persons of another jurisdiction unless otherwise permitted by statute. Follow-up or individualized responses to consumers in a particular state by Live, Learn, Plan in the rendering of personalized investment advice for compensation shall not be made without our first complying with jurisdiction requirements or pursuant to an applicable state exemption.

All written content in this book is for information purposes only. Opinions expressed herein are solely those of Live, Learn, Plan, unless otherwise specifically cited. The material presented is believed to be from reliable sources and no representations are made by our firm as to other parties' informational accuracy or completeness. All information or ideas provided should be discussed in detail with an advisor, accountant, or legal counsel prior to implementation.

CPSIA information can be obtained
at www.ICGtesting.com
Printed in the USA
BVHW071138260522
638205BV00006B/118